Improve Writing Skills For Adults

ENGLISH WRITING CHEATSHEET

Simple, Fun, and Proven Strategies To Impress Anyone In Writing and Comprehension For Essays and Work Reports

JAMES POWERS

Table of Contents

PART I 6

Chapter 1: Understanding Grammatical Structure 7

    The Structure of English 7

    Clauses 8

        Main clause 8

        Subordinate clause 9

        Relative clause 10

        Noun clause 10

    Simple Sentences 12

    Compound Sentences 12

    Complex Sentences 14

    Compound-Complex Sentences 15

Chapter 2: Punctuation 17

    The Period 18

    The Comma 18

    The Apostrophe 19

    The Question Mark 21

    The Exclamation Point 21

    The Quotation Marks 22

    The Semicolon 22

    The Colon 23

Chapter 3: Words for Speaking, not for writing 24

    Spoken English 24

    Written English 25

Chapter 4: Verbs and Tenses 26

    Simple Past Tense 26

    Continuous Past Tense 27

    Perfect Past Tense 27

    Perfect Continuous Past Tense 28

    Simple Present Tense 28

    Continuous Present Tense 29

    Perfect Present Tense 29

    Perfect Continuous Present Tense 30

    Simple Future Tense 30

    Continuous Future Tense 31

    Perfect Future Tense 31

    Perfect Continuous Future Tense 32

Chapter 5: Prepositions 33

    What are Prepositions? 33

    Using Prepositions 33

    The Most Common Prepositions in English 36

        Simple prepositions 37

        Double prepositions 37

        Compound prepositions 38

        Participle prepositions 39

        The most common prepositions 39

PART II 42

Chapter 1: How to Use this Book 43

Chapter 2: 100 Common Nouns to Know 45

What are Nouns? 45

Using Nouns 45

Animal Nouns 46

Directional and Place Nouns 47

People Nouns 48

Career Nouns 50

Weather Nouns 51

Chapter 3: 100 Common Verbs to Know 53

What is a Verb? 53

Using a Verb 53

Active Verbs 53

Feeling Verbs 55

Working Verbs 56

Movement Verbs 57

Chapter 4: 100 Common Adverbs to Know 59

What are Adverbs? 59

Using an Adverb 59

Common Adverbs 60

Chapter 5: 100 Common Adjectives to Know 65

What are Adjectives? 65

Using Adjectives 66

Appearance Adjectives 66

Condition Adjectives 67

Personality Adjectives 68

Quantity Adjectives 68

Sense Adjectives 69

Size and Shape Adjectives 70

Time Adjectives 70

Chapter 6: Commonly Mistaken Words in English 72

Lose and Loose 72

Resign and Re-Sign 73

Advice and Advise 73

Affect and Effect 74

Compliment and Complement 74

Disinterested and Uninterested 75

Wary and Weary 75

Accept and Except 76

Then and Than 76

Their, There, and They're 76

Too, Two, and To 77

Chapter 7: Irregular Verbs 78

Irregular Verbs and Conjugations in English 78

Common Irregular Verbs 79

Chapter 8: Compound Words 85

The Types of Compound Words 86

Closed compounds 86

Open compounds 86

Hyphenated compounds 86

Creating Compound Words 87

Commonly Used Compound Words 87

PART III 90

Chapter 1: Ricky Responsibility 91

Chapter 2: Hannah Learns About Hard Work 93

Chapter 3: Chester Gains His Confidence! 95

Chapter 4: Carly Learns to Communicate 97

Chapter 5: Lester Learns a Lesson About Love 99

Chapter 6: Felicia Spends Time With Family 101

Chapter 7: Sean Gets Sick 102

Chapter 8: Melissa Makes a New Friend 105

Chapter 9: Austin Learns to Care for Animals 108

Chapter 10: Chelsea Discovers Consistency 110

Chapter 11: Barney Becomes Brave 112

Chapter 12: Talia Learns About Team Work 113

PART IV 115

PART I

Chapter 1: Understanding Grammatical Structure

The English language, whether written or spoken, is created upon grammar. Grammar is the set of rules that will control the pattern that is spoken so that everyone understands what is being said. Grammar is what tells us that we say "I went to school" instead of "I school to went" or "School went to I" when you are trying to get something across. Primarily in English, you can expect to see four types of sentences that we will go over now.

The Structure of English

Before we get into the sentence structures themselves, let's talk a bit about English. English syntax, the order that words are given, tells us the order to put our words. In English, syntax usually tells us that we need to speak in subject-verb-object form. This isn't as complicated as it sounds. Let's break down those three words briefly.

Subject refers to the person that does the action. It is the doer—it is the noun that the sentence is based on. For example, if you see the sentence, "I went to school," the word "I" is the subject. I am the one that is doing the thing.

Verb refers to the action, as we have gone over. It is the thing that is done.

Object is the thing that I acted upon. It is the receiver of the verb. Not all sentences will have this. For example, "I play" doesn't have an object, but the sentence "I play ball" does. In that instance, "ball" is the object.

Of course, other modifiers can go into the sentence, such as the adjectives, adverbs, and prepositions, but for the most part, all sentences will typically have the subject, verb, and object.

Clauses

When you have that subject and a verb, you have a complete thought—this is known as a *clause*. Sentences are built upon these clauses; the clauses are the building blocks of the sentence that change the meanings. Clauses have several different forms. These include:

Main clause

Main clauses are always a subject and a verb in that order. They create a thought that is complete all on their own. For example, "I go." This is a complete thought and therefore is the main clause. It can stand as its own sentence alone.

Subordinate clause

Subordinate clauses are a bit more complex. They follow the pattern of subordinate conjunction, subject, and verb. They do not create complete sentences on their own.

Subordinate conjunctions include phrasing such as:

- After
- Even if
- In order to
- Once
- Though
- Unless
- Until
- Wherever
- Whenever
- While

This is not an exhaustive list, but it does include several that are common.

When you have this structure, you have a clause such as:

"Whenever I go"

As you see, this is not a complete thought—you are missing half of the sentence. These clauses need to be paired with others.

Relative clause

A relative clause requires a beginning of a relative pronoun or a relative adverb. These are effective sentences that begin with Who, What, When, Where, Why, or How, as well as anything similar, such as Which, That, or Whose.

These clauses have a pattern of:

Relative pronoun or adverb + subject + verb

Again, you have an incomplete thought. Let's see these in action:

- *Which I do*
- *Where I like to go*
- *What I want*
- *Where he runs*
- *Who finishes things up*

As you can see, these thoughts are only half of a sentence; they don't actually tell you the whole picture.

Noun clause

Finally, let's consider noun clauses for a moment. These are clauses that serve the role of a noun in the sentence. The best way to understand this is through example. Let's say we have the following sentence:

"I like the toppings on this pizza."

You can replace the noun of "toppings" with a noun clause:

"I like what you have put onto the pizza."

As you see, you have replaced the noun with the clause:

"what you have put onto the pizza"

Which is an incomplete thought on its own. That clause does not stand on its own.

Now, let's start putting these clauses together to begin to understand sentence structure.

Simple Sentences

Simple sentences are as simple as the name implies. They are sentences that consist of a single independent or main clause. For example, you can see sentences such as:

- *I didn't study.*
- *He went to the park.*
- *She offered to help.*
- *The dog chews the bone.*
- She ate food.

All of these are short sentences that are broken down and are short. They could be made longer, but they are still complete thoughts on their own without adding anything else. These sentences are typically used by children, English learners, and when there really isn't much more to add to a sentence.

Compound Sentences

Compound sentences start to get a bit more complex. They combine two independent clauses together to create a longer sentence. You can take two sentences and connect them with a conjunction to create something that is longer and conveys more at once. You could also choose to break the sentence down into the two independent clauses as well if you chose to do so, but you are not required.

Conjunctions are connecting words. They are the words that are designed to connect clauses or sentences together in different ways. In English, we have seven of these that are able to be used, and you can remember them with the acronym FANBOYS. These conjunctions are:

- For
- And
- Nor
- But
- Or
- Yet
- So

As you can see, when you write them all out, they spell out the word "Fanboys." These words will be able to connect two clauses together in English, such as:

"I wanted to go to the party, but I got sick."

Notice how this sentence consists of two different sentences? You could remove the conjunction and replace the comma with a period, and you would still have a complete sentence that you could use. You would get "I wanted to go to the party. I got sick." This tells everything that it needed to, but it is more disjointed. It doesn't flow well and sounds more like a child is writing a story. If you want your speech to sound more fluent, you need to make use of compound sentences and vary the sentence structure that you use.

Complex Sentences

Complex sentences bring in clauses and start to make things trickier. Complex sentences are broken down into independent and subordinate clauses. Remember, a subordinate clause is not a complete thought on its own. It needs a leader—the independent or main clause—to help it out. In these sentences, you will see them paired one to one. You will have one independent clause and one of the subordinate forms. For example:

"If I had been more careful, I would not have broken my glass."

"Whenever he runs late, he always makes everyone angry."

"While I enjoy pizza, I like pasta more."

Notice how all of these sentences have one complete thought, and then a modifying thought on them. The subordinate clauses serve to modify the independent thought or add more context. Let's look at that second sentence for a moment. "He always makes everyone angry" is a complete sentence on its own. You see the subject (he) the verb (makes) and the object (everyone) with several other additions thrown in there that we don't need to talk about right this moment. However, the clause itself is independent—it stands even on its own. Now, let's look at that second clause for a moment: "Whenever he runs late," is intended to create a conditional. It specifies when the independent clause plays out. It adds extra context that otherwise wouldn't be there, and you can see that there is more to it than he always makes everyone angry. He only makes everyone angry when he runs late.

Compound-Complex Sentences

Now, let's look at compound-complex sentences. These are the kinds that will include a compound sentence, meaning that you will have two independent clauses that are connected by a conjunction, but you will also have a subordinate clause as well that will bring everything together.

For example:

I really want to buy myself a new book, but I don't have enough money unless I work an extra shift.

This sentence has several parts to it—you can see that there are two independent clauses in there:

1. I really want to buy myself a new book
2. I don't have enough money

Both of those are independent clauses that have been connected by the conjunction of "but."

Then, you have the last part:

3. Unless I work an extra shift

This is an incomplete thought on its own—it is a subordinate clause that needs to be connected to an independent clause. In this sentence, you have the compound and the complex structures put together into one for you to use all together. This is what creates that compound-complex structure.

Chapter 2: Punctuation

When it comes to written English, we need ways to break things up. Words need to be broken down to show the complete ideas wherever they are. You must be able to direct where pauses fall and how sentences come together, after all. To understand why we need punctuation, try to read the following:

I really like to go to school because it is fun to learn new things I really like to read all about different animals and places because there is so much to learn about a world as wide and vast as ours is there are so many different cultures that are so interesting and it is fun to see how everyone around the world likes to do things it can be so different from how we do them at home

Can you read that easily? It all blurs together. Thankfully, we have punctuation to save you from trying to decipher the different clauses. Punctuation is used in writing to allow us to separate out words and sentences into the complete clauses or parts so that we are able to understand the meaning better. Instead of getting something like the above, you can instead get the true meaning:

I really like to go to school because it is fun to learn new things. I really like to read all about different animals and places because there is so much to learn about a world as wide and vast as ours is. There are so many different cultures that are so interesting, and it is fun to see how everyone around the world likes to do things. It can be so different from how we do them at home.

Notice how suddenly that entire paragraph becomes much more understandable just by adding in a few periods and a comma! Punctuation matters, and because of that, let's go over the most common punctuation that you can expect to see in English grammar and writing.

The Period

Periods (.) are used at the end of declarative sentences—sentences that are designed to make a statement without much emphasis or that are not meant to pose a question. They mark the end of that entire sentence so that the individual can move on to whatever comes next. For example:

I really like to read new books.

This reads entirely differently than something that would use a question mark or an exclamation point. It is a calm point that is made and stated matter-of-factly.

The Comma

The comma is used to indicate a pause in a sentence. It shows the separation of elements or ideas in order to maintain the structure. They are used when separating out elements within a list, when you have two complete sentences that are connected by a conjunction, and when you directly address someone else. They are also commonly used in numbers to help break them up, in dates to separate the day from the year, and after the salutation and closing of a letter. For example:

Thanks for helping me today, Mary.

I like to eat my vegetables first, and then enjoy the protein.

I really like the red, green, and blue ones.

The Apostrophe

Apostrophes are used to show that a letter has been left out of a word and when you are talking in the possessive case. These are two very different uses, but both are valid and quite common in English. The apostrophe in a possessive is what shows you that there is ownership between the two nouns. Consider the difference between:

Janie's cat is adorable

And

Janies cat is adorable

Without the apostrophe, you may assume that Janies cat is a type of cat. You need to add in that possessive apostrophe to make it clear for others to understand.

When you use an apostrophe in a word to show the omitting of a letter, you are creating what is known as a *contraction*. Contractions happen when you have two words or one word in some cases, and you omit just one letter to make it less formal. In English, they exist in many different forms. Typically, they will have a very specific pattern to them, such as:

- Let's (let us)
- I'm (I am)
- -'s (is—he's become he is)
- -'ll (will—he'll becomes he will)
- -'d (had/would—I'd becomes I had, or I would)
- -'re (are – We're becomes we are)
- -n't (not—hasn't becomes has not)
- -'ve (have – could've becomes could have)

To use these, you are using something that is usually shortened in speech to make it less formal. However, you must keep in mind that while in speech, it may sound like you're saying "could of," you are actually pronouncing the word "could've," and you need to be mindful of this point.

The Question Mark

A question mark (?) at the end of a sentence is used to create a question. When you stick it there, you usually translate to raising the intonation just slightly in spoken English. You would use it like:

When can I go there?

Could I borrow this?

May I please head out now?

Did they already leave?

The Exclamation Point

Exclamation points (!) are used to show emphasis. They are not typically used in formal writing, but if you are creating a dialog and want to show an outcry or an emphasis on something, this is how you do so. You are trying to really push the point of what you are saying. For example, you might say:

Wow! I'm so glad that I'm done!

That was so cool!

I really like what you've done!

Your new haircut looks great!

The Quotation Marks

Quotation marks ("") surround speech or when you are writing something that is, word for word, identical. It shows that someone has said what is written, whether in your nonfiction context or in other contexts as well. For example,

I walked outside to check the mail and my neighbor said, "Hey, Bob! How's it going?"

In a written report, any quotes that you use or any time you use someone's exact words, you put them into the quotation marks.

The Semicolon

A semicolon is a tricky bit of punctuation that people tend to get wrong. Its job is to connect independent clauses without requiring a conjunction word. Effectively, the semicolon will eliminate the need for that conjunction so that you are able to show a closer relationship between the two clauses. For example:

I really like what you are wearing; I would have preferred it if it were green instead of blue though.

He was really frustrated; he knew that getting a new job was for the best, but he was still annoyed at the process.

The Colon

A colon has three primary uses. It can introduce a list, it can show independent clauses that connect together a bit differently than a semicolon, or it can be used for emphasis. All of these have their own roles and times and places—they all are important in different ways. For example:

I really enjoy listening to all kinds of music: Rock, rap, hip-hop, and even classical.

I know that my grade is set in stone at this point: I can't fail even if I don't take the final because my grade is so high already.

My favorite thing in the world is simple: My cat.

Chapter 3: Words for Speaking, not for writing

When it comes to English, there are primarily two forms—the way that you communicate in writing is different than when you speak, and it becomes imperative for you to understand the difference. Primarily, the major difference is that spoken language is far less formal. Written English, especially when you are writing a formal paper or email, is written with much more adherence to the rules, and if you want to be as effective as possible with your communication, understanding the difference between the two is imperative. Let's go over the primary difference between the two now.

Spoken English

Spoken English will be far more informal. It is also much more likely to contain slang—informal language that is used to convey a meaning that is understood by your peers. However, slang should never be included in anything formal. While the party you went to may have been "lit," the event that you are writing about for school most certainly was not. It is okay for you to use slang when you are speaking. When it comes to looking at spoken English, you should expect to see the following:

- Personal pronouns
- Shorter thoughts
- Greater repetition of words or phrases
- Colloquial words and contractions

- Familiar words
- Less references to earlier stated information
- Logical structure
- Cohesion to the content
- Varied speech patterns

Written English

Written English is typically reserved for more formality. The formality that goes into writing is necessary, and it is often found in academic or business settings. Because written English is preserved, it is usually fine-tuned to be as perfect as possible. This is necessary and essential—you have to be able to convey your ideas well so that they can be understood. In written English you can expect to see the following:

- Less personal pronoun usage
- Sentence structures that are naturally more complex
- Repetition through the use of varying language
- Formal tone without the use of colloquial language
- Precise vocabulary so that you can use as few words as possible
- Precise language despite the audience
- May include references to previously discussed information
- Cohesion and fluid arguments

Chapter 4: Verbs and Tenses

We know that verbs are action words. We know that they have very important roles that they play. However, it is time that we start talking about how verbs can be conjugated. Conjugation is the change of the verb's form to create a clearer meaning. This is why you can take a verb such as "accept," and you can change it to clearly show the context and the subject, as well as the tense. Accept can become accepts, accepted, or accepting as well. It changes based on the tense that it is in.

Within this chapter, we are going to go over all 12 of the tenses that are present in English and how you can create them with regular verbs—verbs that don't change between tenses, such as eat and swim.

Simple Past Tense

This tense is simple—it shows that something has already concluded at some other point in time prior to now. It shows something in the past that finished in the past.

Conjugation pattern:

I, you, we, they, he, she, it: accepted (infinitive + ed)

Continuous Past Tense

Continuous past tense is used to show that there were two actions that occurred—one happened in the past and was not finished, and another completed action interrupted it.

Conjugation pattern:

I, he, she, it: *was accepting when they rejected it.* (was infinitive + ing)

He, she, it: *were accepting when they rejected it.* (were infinitive + ing)

Perfect Past Tense

The perfect past tense is important to show that two things happened at the same time, and the first action finishes before the second occurs.

Conjugation pattern:

I, you, we, they, he, she, it: *had accepted the news when they learned something new* (had infinitive +ed)

Perfect Continuous Past Tense

This isn't used very often at all, but you may run into it in textbooks or writing. It shows that there was a complete action that happened before a second event happened, and you describe how long it had occurred.

Conjugation pattern:

I, you, we, they, he, she, it: had been accepting for a long time before it got popular (had been infinitive + ing)

Simple Present Tense

Simple present tense is for something that is routine—it tells the listener that you regularly do something, or you may never do it. For example, "I never run." Or "I play piano." You aren't giving much detail, but it is just enough to clarify that you do something sometimes.

Conjugation pattern:

I, you, we, they: accept (infinitive of the verb)

He, she, it: accepts (infinitive of the verb + s)

Continuous Present Tense

Continuous present tense allows you to describe what you are doing right this moment. You are talking about something that is currently happening or is something that has not yet finished.

Conjugation pattern:

I: am accepting right now (am infinitive + -ing)

You, we, they: are accepting right now (are infinitive + ing)

He, she, it: is accepting right now (is infinitive + ing)

Perfect Present Tense

Perfect present tense changes things up just a bit. It is commonly mistaken with a simple present, but in this case, you are showing that something has been completed already. Whatever it was is done now.

Conjugation pattern:

I, you, we, they: have accepted (have infinitive + ed)

He, she, it: has accepted (has infinitive + ed)

Perfect Continuous Present Tense

This next tense shows that something started in the past but is still happening in the present. It is something that you are still actively performing, even though it already began.

Conjugation pattern:

I, you, we, they: have been accepting (have been infinitive + ing)

He, she, it: has been accepting (has been infinitive + ing)

Simple Future Tense

The simple future tense is all about something that will happen in the future—you are talking about something that may happen tomorrow or in an hour from now. You can also use "going to" instead of "will."

Conjugation pattern:

I, you, we, they, he, she, it: will accept it tomorrow (will + infinitive)

Or

I: am going to accept it tomorrow (am going to + infinitive)

You, we, they: are going to accept it tomorrow (are going to + infinitive)

He, she, it: is going to accept it tomorrow (is going to + infinitive)

Continuous Future Tense

The continuous future tense is designed to show that something is not complete when something else happens. It is like the continuous past, but in the future instead.

Conjugation pattern:

I, you, we, they, he, she, it: will be accepting when the time comes. (will be infinitive + ing)

Perfect Future Tense

The perfect future tense is meant to show that an action must be completed before the other is completed.

Conjugation pattern:

I, you, we, they, he, she, it: will have accepted things by the time that you call.

Perfect Continuous Future Tense

This shows that there is an event that happens while another happens at the same time. It is usually used to convey a sense of time for clarity.

Conjugation pattern:

I, you, we, they, he, she, it: will have been accepting for a while before you call: (will have been infinitive + ing)

Chapter 5: Prepositions

What are Prepositions?

In the English language, prepositions are required to ensure that you can convey the right meaning. They make the difference between knowing whether something is above or below something, or whether someone is something for or against a cause. There is so much in the English language that can't just be conveyed through nouns and verbs—sometimes you need prepositions to precede a noun or pronoun to show its relationship to another word. Using prepositions is essential if you want to create clear sentences that will convey the most possible information about a topic. If you want to be able to convey that you walk to school instead of from school, you need prepositions. If you want to be able to convey that you work with money rather than for money, you need to have the right preposition.

The English language has many different prepositions—150, to be exact, and they are incredibly important. While other languages can get away with less, those prepositions usually entail several of the English ones. If you want to be able to use these prepositions, you will need to first know what they are and what they do.

Using Prepositions

Using prepositions doesn't have to be difficult. They do require you, however, to understand what the object of a preposition is. The object of a preposition is the word that follows after it. Because prepositions show and connect ideas between two things, they must be paired with something. It is essential for there to be the second object that is being modified.

For example, let's take the preposition "with." Using that preposition, let's come up with a simple sentence to use for demonstrative purposes:

I cook with care.

Care is the object of the preposition there, meaning that the word "with" is there to connect cook and care. With is the preposition that connects and relates the two words together, modifying them both. You can't say, "I cook care." That means that you are actively cooking care—which you can't do. However, when you modify it with the word "with," you are able to make it clear that instead of cooking care, you are carefully cooking.

Prepositions are used in what are known as prepositional phrases—they consist of a preposition and the object of a preposition, along with any modifiers, such as adjectives, that you may have included. Typically, this will serve to create an adjective or an adverb for your sentence in one prepositional phrase. For example, you can use a prepositional phrase as:

It is a card from Frank.

The prepositional phrase here, "from Frank," serves as an adjective; it describes the card. However, you can also choose to create an adverb instead:

Frank sent the card from France.

Here, the prepositional phrase, "from France," serves as a modifier for the verb. It describes what was sent, making it an adverb. Since it modifies the meaning of the verb, you get a prepositional adverb.

Keep in mind that when using your prepositional phrases, it is commonly recommended that you avoid ending a sentence in them. Prepositions should not be the last word in a sentence because they must be followed by a noun. Of course, in spoken English, no one will think twice of you saying, "That's something I never thought of," but in writing, that may be deemed a bit too informal. Instead, it is recommended that you reword the sentence, so you say, "I never thought of that."

Additionally, a common problem that people have with their prepositions is unintentionally using the wrong case after they have finished a sentence. In English, you must follow a preposition with the objective case. That means that your pronouns will become me, him, her, us, and them. This is just the rule of English, but it throws some people off. Instead of writing,

This is a card from my wife and I

You would write,

This is a card from my wife and me.

You must remember that you will use "me" following a prepositional phrase. The best way to remember this is to try eliminating the other person from the sentence to make sure that you get it right. Instead of "This is a card from I," you would get "This is a card from me," so it is only natural that you list it as "from my wife and me." It might be a bit tricky at first, but with practice, you can get it down simply.

The Most Common Prepositions in English

The English language has five different types of prepositions that you will need to know so that you can use them effectively. If you want to be able to convey the meanings that you want to get across clearly, you need prepositions. Let's go over those five types of prepositions now.

Simple prepositions

Simple prepositions will show you a time, place, or location. There are many different words that will do this for you, including:

- Above
- At
- By
- Down
- For
- From
- In
- Near
- Off
- On
- Over
- Since
- Through
- To
- Under
- With

These are meant to convey a meaning or describe something rather than conveying a change to something. For example, you went over a mountain, or you worked with a friend.

Double prepositions

Some prepositions are double prepositions—they take two simple prepositions and use them together to indicate the direction that is being used in the sentence. They allow you to get extra meaning through words and phrases such as:

- Atop
- From within
- Into
- Onto
- Out of
- Up to
- Upon
- Without

Notice how all of these work to provide you with extra meaning—you are atop a tree rather than up a tree. It is more specific. The baby didn't climb on the table—he climbed onto it. These are commonly used when you have direction or change in a sentence.

Compound prepositions

Compound prepositions are more complex—they usually involve two or more words that are combined, with one of them typically being a simple preposition with the other word being something that is specified. These allow you to convey location when you are talking about something. Some complex prepositions include:

- According to
- Across from
- Aside from
- Form beneath
- In addition to

- In front of
- In the middle of
- On behalf of

Participle prepositions

Participle prepositions are those that have endings such as –ed or –ing that serve the purpose of a preposition. These allow you to convey extra meaning as well. They include words such as:

- Concerning
- Considering
- During
- Following
- Including
- Regarding

The most common prepositions

If you want to know what the most common prepositions are, there is a simple way to remember them. Think about all the places a mouse can go, and that is your list. This will help you to remember that prepositions are designed to show a relationship between two words through specifying their location relative to each other or how they interact.

By learning most of the common prepositions, you will put yourself in a position of better understanding everything that you need to do—you will make it clear to yourself what comes next naturally in your writing, and you will teach yourself which case you need to use afterward as well. Learning the prepositions will help you greatly in making sure that you are able to keep your grammar on track, on point, and understandable for everyone else.

The most common prepositions then include:

- Above
- Across
- After
- Around
- At
- Before
- Behind
- Below
- Beside
- Between
- By
- Down
- During
- For
- From
- In
- Inside
- Of
- Off
- On
- Onto

- Out
- Through
- To
- Under
- Up
- With

Keep in mind that this is a short list—there are 150, after all, but as someone just starting out, these are the most important ones that you will need to know if you want to be effective in your conversations. When you have these ones memorized, everything else comes easily as a direct result, and you won't have to worry so much about what you are doing. It eventually becomes like a sort of grammatical muscle memory—you will be able to predict what to say and naturally through plenty of practice and trial and error.

PART II

Chapter 1: How to Use this Book

So, you're working on learning or bettering your English grammar. You're in the right place! If you are here, you're looking for a simple guide that will easily teach you the rules of English grammar. This book will also provide you with all sorts of new vocabulary words to use that will help you to convey better what you wish to when speaking or writing.

As you use this book, you are going to be presented first with the most common categories of words—nouns, verbs, adverbs, and adjectives. As you read through these chapters, you will be given 100 words to learn and use in your own sentences. The words that are provided will be those that will serve you well if you hope to travel or speak in English regularly. Use these chapters as a sort of vocabulary booster.

Then, as you continue, you will see words that are a bit less common or intuitive. We will go over some words that are irregular or are not likely to follow the patterns that you are accustomed to. These words might not follow the rules but are still important to learn and know. Think of this as teaching you the most common exceptions so that you will know what to look out for.

Finally, you will be given a crash-course in making sure that your English is impeccable. You will want to take the time to go over these chapters slowly and carefully. Don't feel the need to rush into them. Practice the conjugation patterns in these chapters. Work on using the punctuation better. Focus on the differences between written and spoken English.

By using these tools in these manners, you will discover that English doesn't have to be as difficult as you may expect it, and you will be able to brush up on skills that may have eluded you in the past- but you can master them. All you have to do is try.

Chapter 2: 100 Common Nouns to Know

What are Nouns?

Nouns are simply put, people, places, or things. They are things that can do things or can have things done to them. Everything that we talk about or see has a name; the name of something is the noun. The noun is the naming word for something.

Typically, nouns are things that we can touch or things that we want to objectify, even if they are abstract. They allow us to talk about the things that they are. They come in all sorts of forms and are either common or proper. Common nouns are words for things. They are definitions—they tell anyone what something is.

We also have proper nouns—the names for very specific things. So, while girls may refer to all people that are women or female, you can also name one specific girl: Betty. You can specify this with a proper noun, which names one specific thing within a general category of things.

Using Nouns

Nouns are used either as subjects or objects in English—they are the things that do the acting or are acted upon. For example: "The dog ate." The dog is the noun here—and it is the subject. It is doing the thing. When you add an object to the sentence as well, such as "The dog ate a bone." The dog, being the subject, acted upon the bone, which is also a noun.

Animal Nouns

1. **Herd:** Several hoofed mammals that live together as one group, commonly used for livestock.
2. **Pack:** Several animals that work together in one group with a leader, typically hunters such as wolves
3. **Amphibian:** Coldblooded animals that live in both the land and in the water, such as frogs, salamanders, and newts.
4. **Reptile:** Coldblooded animals that are scaly and lay soft-shelled eggs on the land, such as turtles, lizards, and snakes.
5. **Mammal:** Warm-blooded animals with fur or hair that provide milk to their babies, such as people, dogs, and rabbits.
6. **Flock:** A group of animals that are commonly herded by either a person or by a leader.
7. **Habitat:** Somewhere that animals live.
8. **Hibernate:** A period of extended sleep, typically over the winter, to survive when there is less food available.
9. **Carnivore:** Animals that eat only meat to survive.
10. **Herbivore:** Animals that eat only plants to survive.
11. **Insectivore:** Animals that eat only insects to survive.
12. **Omnivore:** Animals that eat both plants and animals to survive.
13. **Litter:** A group of baby animals from the same mother, typically used for cats, dogs, and other mammals.

14. **Territory:** The area that the animal lives and recognizes as its own home.
15. **Venom:** Poison that an animal is capable of injecting straight into the body and bloodstream of someone or something else, such as through biting and stinging.
16. **Poison:** Poison that is excreted in other ways that must be consumed by the other animal, typically through the skin, to make the other animal think that eating it would be a bad idea.
17. **Maw:** Another word for a mouth, typically a longer one that has plenty of teeth.
18. **Prey:** The animal that has been hunted for food.
19. **Quadruped:** An animal that walks on four feet or legs.
20. **Biped:** An animal that walks on two feet or legs.

Directional and Place Nouns

1. **North:** The direction that a compass needle will point toward, meaning toward the North Pole.
2. **East:** The direction to the left of where a compass needle is pointing.
3. **South:** The direction opposite of North.
4. **West:** The direction to the right of where a compass needle will point.
5. **Left:** The thing to the west when you face north.
6. **Right:** The thing to the east when you face south.
7. **Up:** The thing that is above you.
8. **Down:** The thing that is below you.
9. **Here:** The thing that is right near you at that point in time.

10. **There:** The thing that you are directing attention toward further away.
11. **Over there:** Something that you are directing toward that is even further away.
12. **Outside:** Something that is on the external side of something—it is not protected or shielded.
13. **Inside:** Something that is internal—it is covered or protected by something.
14. **Straight:** Something that is directly in front without curving or turning away.
15. **Park:** A large area that is used for recreation; typically, it is highly planted.
16. **Garden:** A small area that is used for growing plants, typically in fruits, vegetables, or flowers.
17. **Parking Lot:** An area where you can park your car temporarily while you go somewhere.
18. **Library:** A room that is filled with books and periodicals that can be borrowed.
19. **Store:** Somewhere that you can make purchases for new objects.
20. **Mountain:** A naturally elevated area at the top of a steep hill that is typically higher.

People Nouns

1. **Friend**: Someone who has a bond of mutual affection with someone else—not family or romantic.
2. **Crowd:** A large group of people, typically consisting of several smaller groups.

3. **Party:** One group of people, typically used when reserving groceries.
4. **Team:** A group of people all working toward the same end goal.
5. **Leader:** The person that's taking charge of a group to lead everyone toward the same goal.
6. **Student:** Someone who is spending time studying to learn something, typically in college.
7. **Helper:** Someone who is willing to assist someone else in trying to do something.
8. **Group:** Several people together all working toward the same thing.
9. **Acquaintance:** Someone that you know in passing but don't really know them well.
10. **Enemy:** Someone who is actively against what you need to do.
11. **Champion:** Someone who has come out on top in a competition, typically in sports.
12. **Winner:** Someone who has won something.
13. **Loser:** Someone who has lost something, or it can be used as an insult.
14. **Roommate:** Someone that lives with someone else without being in a romantic relationship or familial unit
15. **Employee:** Someone who works somewhere at a certain job.
16. **Gentleman:** A polite way to refer to a man in a formal setting.
17. **Boyfriend:** A romantic partner (not married) that is a man.
18. **Girlfriend:** A romantic partner (not married) that is a woman.
19. **Husband:** A married partner that is a man.
20. **Wife:** A married partner that is a woman.

Career Nouns

1. **Doctor:** Someone who works to practice medicine.
2. **Nurse:** Someone who works to provide medical care to the patient.
3. **Accountant:** Someone who works to keep finances in order.
4. **Artist:** Someone who creates art.
5. **Driver:** Someone who drives regularly.
6. **Attendant:** Someone who provides s certain kind of service in a certain context, such as a flight attendant providing services on a plane.
7. **Cashier:** Someone whose job is to ring up purchases and process the transaction.
8. **Teacher:** Someone who teaches children in a school setting.
9. **Police Officer:** Someone who is responsible for enforcing the law.
10. **Firefighter:** Someone who puts out fires when they start to protect people.
11. **Insurance agent:** Someone who processes and manages insurance accounts.
12. **Professor:** The highest-ranking teacher in a university setting.
13. **Scientist:** Someone who researches science.
14. **Veterinarian:** A doctor for animals.
15. **Stocker:** Someone who stocks the shelves at a store.
16. **Psychologist:** An expert that specializes in the working of the mind.
17. **Judge:** Someone whose job is to decide whether the law is being upheld in the courts.
18. **Writer:** Someone who writes for a career.

19. **President:** The leader or governing individual over a company or country, typically through being elected.
20. **Government worker:** Someone who works for the government.

Weather Nouns

1. **Sun:** The star around which the sun orbits that provides warmth and light.
2. **Cloud:** Condensed water vapor in the atmosphere
3. **Precipitation:** Rainwater that falls from the clouds when it gets heavy or cold enough.
4. **Tornado:** A storm filled with violently rotating winds that create the shape of a funnel and move along the ground—they are typically quite destructive.
5. **Gust:** A strung burst of wind.
6. **Icicle:** Frozen pieces of ice formed by dripping water that hang and get a tapered effect.
7. **Forecast:** The prediction for weather for the next several days or weeks based on patterns and radar.
8. **Fog:** Low-lying clouds that create low visibility on the ground.
9. **Snow:** Frozen water vapor that falls in small flakes.
10. **Rainbow:** Colors that shine in the sky when sunlight goes through the water droplets in the sky just right.
11. **Drought:** A period of time where there is no rain when things are dry, and there's a shortage of water.
12. **Flood:** Water that has fallen beyond what is normally contained, creating overflow onto land that is typically not covered in water.

13. **Blizzard:** A heavy, severe snowstorm that typically also includes high winds and lowered visibility.
14. **Hurricane:** A large storm that is characterized by strong, violent winds that begin in the Caribbean.
15. **Fahrenheit:** A measurement for temperature that is typically reserved for use in the US—water freezes at 32 degrees and boils at 212 degrees.
16. **Celsius:** A measurement for temperature that is used worldwide where water freezes at 0 and boils at 100 degrees.
17. **Thermometer:** A tool that is used to measure temperature.
18. **Flurry:** A small swirl of snow caused by a gust of wind.
19. **Breeze:** A light blow of wind.
20. **Humidity:** The measurement of water in the air.

Chapter 3: 100 Common Verbs to Know

What is a Verb?

Verbs are things that you do. A verb is any sort of action that you perform when it is expressed in a word. We have all sorts of words that can describe what we do, and they can be as colorful or descriptive as you want them to be. For example, you may have "I ran" as a sentence. You did something—you ran. However, you can make it more specific than that, too. "I sprinted." "I jogged." They all carry different connotations, and they work to paint a clearer picture that can be used as well. To use a verb is essential in a sentence, and you will need to be able to conjugate them. This chapter is going to focus primarily on simple verbs that do not conjugate in strange manners—which we will address later.

Using a Verb

Using a verb is simple—it involves you conjugating your verb into the right case to get what you want. We will be going into the different conjugation forms when you get to Chapter 12: Verbs and Tenses, and if you want to understand how to conjugate the verbs that you will see here, you will want to go there.

Active Verbs

1. **Cook:** To prepare food to eat.

2. **Work:** To engage in activity to create a desired result.
3. **Make:** To create something.
4. **Pay:** To give money or other currency in return for something that was done for you.
5. **Speak:** To say words to tell someone information.
6. **Arrange:** To organize something in a different order, or to set everything in motion.
7. **Answer:** To provide an answer back after someone has asked a question.
8. **Color:** To add color to something.
9. **Cough:** To expel the air from one's lungs forcefully.
10. **Listen:** To actively pay attention to what someone else is saying or the sounds in one's environment.
11. **Jump:** To push off of a surface into the air.
12. **Run:** To actively move quicker than walking.
13. **Shop:** To purchase something to buy goods.
14. **Read:** To look at all of the meanings of written material.
15. **Write:** To put down thoughts onto paper to convey a message or meaning.
16. **Draw:** To create art through the use of making marks and lines.
17. **Talk:** To speak to someone in order to convey meanings.
18. **Plan:** To begin thinking about what will happen in the future to be prepared.
19. **Sit:** To take a position in which one's weight is on one's bottom instead of feet.
20. **Paint:** To put a thin coating onto a surface to add in colors.

Feeling Verbs

1. **Cry:** To shed tears when sad, hurting, or distress.
2. **Laugh:** To make sounds of happiness and amusement.
3. **Like:** To find something enjoyable.
4. **Hate:** To find something unenjoyable.
5. **Love:** To feel deeply attached to something or someone, romantic or otherwise.
6. **Smile:** To show expression with the mouth turned upwards to expose the teeth in a kind, happy look.
7. **Forget:** To fail to remember something.
8. **Learn:** To gain new skills or knowledge.
9. **Choose:** To pick something out
10. **Concern:** To be worried about or to relate to something.
11. **Doubt:** To feel uncertain about something.
12. **Dislike:** To feel annoyed or disapproving of something.
13. **Loathe:** To feel intense disapproval or dislike of something.
14. **Prefer:** To want something more than you want anything else.
15. **Respect:** To deeply admire someone or something based on their achievements.
16. **Frown:** To express displeasure by turning down the mouth's corners.
17. **Focus:** To pay closer attention to something.
18. **Motivate:** To feel drive toward completing a task.
19. **Encourage:** To provide support or hope to someone through actions.
20. **Cheer:** To encourage through praise and joyous expression.

Working Verbs

1. **Build:** To create or construct something through putting the parts together.
2. **Treat:** To take care of someone or something.
3. **Prepare:** To make or plan to get ready for something that will happen in the future.
4. **Sell:** To trade an object for money.
5. **Trade:** To give someone something in exchange for something else.
6. **Negotiate:** To talk with someone else to come to an agreement that both people are happy with.
7. **Gain:** To obtain something or to increase the amount of something that you have.
8. **Improve:** To make something better through working on it.
9. **Boost:** To help something improve over time.
10. **Influence:** To have an effect on something else through your own actions.
11. **Integrate:** To combine things together to create something new that is better than the two parts on their own.
12. **Teach:** To provide instruction to someone else to explain how to do something new.
13. **Advise:** To provide insight or suggestions to the best possible plan of action to someone else.
14. **Resolve:** To find a solution to a problem or dispute that has occurred.
15. **Brief:** To provide information to someone else about how to deal with something.

16. **Edit:** To make revisions to something else to ensure that it is appropriately put together.
17. **Promote:** To actively encourage something, or to further its progress through your support.
18. **Authorize:** To provide active support or approval to do something.
19. **Succeed:** To do something that achieves the end goal that you had.
20. **Search:** To seek out something or to look for something.

Movement Verbs

1. **Walk:** To move at an average pace through lifting and setting both feet up and down without them both being up at the same time.
2. **Turn:** To move in a direction that is different from the one that you are currently walking in.
3. **Bike:** To ride on a bicycle in a pedaling motion.
4. **Drive:** To operate a vehicle through controlling the speed and direction.
5. **Ride:** To sit on something and then control the movement of it. Typically in the context of a vehicle or an animal such as a horse.
6. **Help:** To offer aid in something by offering resources or actions.
7. **Move:** To go in a specific direction or to adjust one's position.
8. **Bolt:** To run quickly.
9. **Skip:** To move in a direction in a bouncy or hopping fashion.
10. **Sprint:** To run with a sudden burst of speed that usually can only be maintained for a short period.

11. **Strut:** To walk in a way that is upright and stiff, usually with an arrogant context.
12. **Leap:** To jump forcefully over a long way or height.
13. **Shrug:** To raise and drop one's shoulders to express that you are uncertain or indifferent about something.
14. **Tap:** To gently touch with a quick, light strike to someone without intent of hurting.
15. **Take:** To receive something from someplace.
16. **Drop:** To let go of something and allow it to fall.
17. **Bend:** To shape or force something that was once straight into a curve.
18. **Flip:** To turn something over suddenly.
19. **Lift:** To raise something up from where it was before.
20. **Twist:** To bend or turn something that was stationary, so it faces a different direction.

Chapter 4: 100 Common Adverbs to Know

What are Adverbs?

Verbs can be modified easily as well. You don't have to just run—you can run quickly, slowly, awkwardly, or even haphazardly. There are a million different ways that you can describe your verbs, and you want to be able to clarify what they are when you do them. Adverbs help you to do that. An adverb is an adjective for a verb—it describes or modifies the verb that you are trying to describe differently. They can be fancy, or they can be simple. However, no matter what they are, they are designed to give you a broader picture of what you are doing.

Using an Adverb

Using adverbs is simple—you just pair an adjective with –ly and then put it into the sentence that you are modifying. For example, if you want to talk about running quickly, you can create sentences such as:

I quickly ran after my friend.

I run quickly.

I run with my dog quickly

As you can see, you can put your adverb in several different places, but the safest bet is almost always just before it. When you do that, you can know that you are on the right track.

As you will notice in the list below, some adverbs still influence or alter the verb of the sentence but do not end in –ly. This is because adverbs will alter one of four things:

1. **Adverbs of manner:** These tell you how the action has happened, such as "I ran quickly." Quickly is the adverb.
2. **Adverbs of place:** These tell you where the verb has occurred, such as, "You walked upstairs." Upstairs is the adverb.
3. **Adverbs of time:** These will tell you when something has happened, such as "I went to the store again." Again is the adverb.
4. **Adverbs of frequency:** These tell you how often something has happened, such as "I read books daily." Daily is the adverb.

Common Adverbs

1. **Absently:** To do something distractedly.
2. **Actually:** To show that something is truthful or factual.
3. **Adoringly:** To do something lovingly or affectionately.
4. **Adventurously:** To do something bravely or without fear of trying something new.
5. **Adversely:** To do something in a way that holds back success or makes the situation unfavorable.
6. **Afterward:** To do something at a later point in time.
7. **Almost:** To not quite, but nearly happen.

8. **Always:** To do something during all occasions.
9. **Angrily:** To do something with a threatening demeanor, or to do something due to anger.
10. **Awkwardly:** To do something in a way that shows unease or embarrassment.
11. **Badly:** To do something in a way that is unsatisfactory or inadequate.
12. **Beautifully:** To do something in an aesthetically pleasing way.
13. **Before:** To something prior to the time being discussed, or in front of someone.
14. **Better:** To do something with increased skill.
15. **Bravely:** To do something despite the potential pain or danger that may be endured.
16. **Briskly:** To do something quickly and energetically.
17. **Broadly:** To do something widely or openly, or to do something generally.
18. **Brutally:** To do something violently or savagely.
19. **Busily:** To do something very actively.
20. **Carefully:** To do something, being mindful to do the details just right.
21. **Clearly:** To do something accurately or in a way that is without doubt.
22. **Coolly:** To do something without enthusiasm or excitement.
23. **Down:** To do something underneath something else.
24. **Downward** To do something that moves down.
25. **Effortlessly:** To do something easily, or as if it were not difficult at all.
26. **Elegantly:** To do something in a graceful way.
27. **Equally:** To do something to the same extent.

28. **Especially:** To put an emphasis on something.
29. **Even:** To emphasize something that is extreme or surprising.
30. **Eventually:** To do something in the end or after a delay.
31. **Everywhere:** To do something in every location.
32. **Extremely:** To do something to a very great degree.
33. **Far:** To do something in the distance.
34. **Fast:** To do something rapidly or quickly.
35. **Fervently:** To do something passionately or with heartfelt feelings.
36. **Fiercely:** To do something with intensity.
37. **Foolishly:** To do something stupidly or unwisely.
38. **Gently:** To do something tenderly or carefully to avoid harming.
39. **Gracefully:** To do something with beauty or elegance.
40. **Halfheartedly:** To do something without giving it the deserved effort.
41. **Happily:** To do something enjoyably, without complaint or disagreement.
42. **Hard:** To do something that is difficult.
43. **Here:** To do something in the current location.
44. **Honestly:** To do something truthfully.
45. **Innocently:** To do something without guilt or in a way that is morally acceptable.
46. **Inquisitively:** To do something in a manner of being curious about something.
47. **Instantly:** To do something immediately or without delay.
48. **Intensely:** To do something in a serious way or with extreme force.
49. **Irritably:** To do something in a way that conveys irritation.
50. **Joyously:** To do something happily.

51. **Knowledgably:** To do something while being well informed of the situation.
52. **Lazily:** To do something haphazardly, or as if you do not care.
53. **Loyally:** To do something in a way that shows one's allegiance or support toward a situation.
54. **Madly:** To do something intensely to show passion, or conveying a sense of insanity.
55. **Meaningfully:** To do something with significance or full of meaning or purpose.
56. **Obediently:** To do something without argument after being asked to do so.
57. **Obnoxiously:** To do something in an annoying manner.
58. **Often:** To do something regularly, but not all the time.
59. **Openly:** To do something without trying to conceal or hide it.
60. **Playfully:** to do something in a lighthearted manner.
61. **Poorly:** To do something unskillfully.
62. **Quickly:** To do something rapidly.
63. **Quietly:** To do something without making much noise.
64. **Quite:** To do something completely or to a significant extent.
65. **Randomly:** To do something indiscriminately.
66. **Rapidly:** To do something quickly.
67. **Recklessly:** To do something without caring about the consequences.
68. **Rightfully:** To do something legitimately.
69. **Seemingly:** To do something that gives the impression of having a certain quality.
70. **Sleepily:** To do something in a manner that conveys tiredness or like one is about to fall asleep.
71. **Slowly:** To do something at a not quick pace.

72. **Smoothly:** To do something without problems, or to make something continually flowing.
73. **Soon:** To do something in the near future.
74. **Sternly:** To do something seriously or authoritatively.
75. **Supposedly:** To do something according to the general assumptions or beliefs, typically conveying doubt toward the veracity of a statement.
76. **Surprisingly:** To do something unexpectedly or with unexpected results.
77. **Sweetly:** To do something with kindness.
78. **Terribly:** To do something extremely or unpleasantly.
79. **Tomorrow:** To do something the next day.
80. **Too:** To do something as well or, in addition, or to do something to an excessive degree.
81. **Triumphantly:** To do something in a way that conveys victory or achievement.
82. **Unabashedly:** To do something in an unembarrassed way.
83. **Unbearably:** To do something in a way that is hard to endure.
84. **Unethically:** To do something that is morally questionable.
85. **Unexpectedly:** To do something that is surprising or has surprising results.
86. **Upward:** To do something in the direction of up.
87. **Urgently:** To do something in a manner that is immediate or attentive.
88. **Vacantly:** To do something without paying much attention to it.
89. **Vaguely:** To do something unclearly.
90. **Vainly:** To do something to no avail, or to do something with an excessive appraisal of one's ability.
91. **Valiantly:** To do something with determination.

92. **Very:** To do something extremely.
93. **Vicariously:** To do something through imagining yourself as someone else.
94. **Warily:** To do something on guard or suspiciously.
95. **Wearily:** To do something tiredly.
96. **Well:** To do something with exceptional skill.
97. **Wildly:** To do something in an uncontrolled manner.
98. **Worriedly:** To do something out of concern.
99. **Yearly:** Something that occurs on an annual basis.
100. **Yesterday:** Something that was done the day prior.

Chapter 5: 100 Common Adjectives to Know

What are Adjectives?

Adjectives are words that are meant to describe something else. They are designed to alter the understanding of a noun or provide more information about the noun that they are describing. Typically, nouns and pronouns are modified to convey more information. It is the difference between saying the dog and the nice dog, or the angry dog. It conveys more information that needs to be known so that the message can be as clear as possible.

Typically, adjectives come before a noun, which is known as a predicative adjective. However, there are also postpositive adjectives—those that come afterward. Usually, the postpositive adjectives are used for pronouns, while typically, predicative adjectives are nouns.

Using Adjectives

To use an adjective, all you have to do is put it either before the noun or after the pronoun, depending upon the adjective. For example, you could have: "The kind person" or "Someone kind." Other than that, there isn't much that you have to do to change it.

If you want to create an adjective, you can do so by adding –ing to a verb and putting it before a noun as well. For example, a smiling child, or someone smiling. This is another way to make use of adjectives in a way that can change up your writing.

Appearance Adjectives

1. **Attractive:** Something that is aesthetically pleasing and draws you toward it.
2. **Beautiful:** Something that is aesthetically pleasing and attractive.
3. **Blemished:** Something that is tarnished or damaged in appearance.
4. **Bright:** Something that looks quite lit or colorful.
5. **Clean:** Something that is kept free from dirt or stains.
6. **Dark:** Something that is dim or hard to see.
7. **Dimpled:** Something that is bumpy.
8. **Dusty:** Something that is covered in dirt or dust.
9. **Fuzzy:** Something that is fluffy or frayed in appearance, or is vague and difficult to understand.

10. **Jagged:** Something that is rough or sharp on the edge.
11. **Luxurious:** Something that is extremely comfortable or elegant.
12. **Rough:** Something that is unfinished or unpolished, or has been damaged.
13. **Smooth:** Something that is even and regular in consistency without lumps or edges.
14. **Soft:** Something that is easy to mold and is pleasing or subtle.
15. **Ugly**: Something that is aesthetically unpleasing.

Condition Adjectives

1. **Abrasive:** Something that is rough or irritating.
2. **Advanced:** Something that is difficult or something not for beginners.
3. **Annoying:** Something that is irritating.
4. **Better:** Something that is more excellent than something else.
5. **Boring:** Something that is dull or uninteresting.
6. **Busy:** Something that is active.
7. **Cautious:** Something that is careful.
8. **Clever:** Something that is intelligent or quick to understand.
9. **Disturbing:** Something that is worrying, concerning, or causing anxiety.
10. **Frail:** Something that is fragile and weak.
11. **Horrible:** Something that is shocking or very unpleasant.
12. **Irritating:** Something that is annoying.
13. **Maddening:** Something that is frustrating.
14. **Poor:** Something that is worse than expected or desirable, or is lacking in money or standards.

15. **Tedious:** Something that is monotonous or dull.

Personality Adjectives

1. **Ambitious:** Showing determination to succeed.
2. **Caring:** Showing kindness and wanting to help others.
3. **Confident:** Showing an air of competence.
4. **Congenial:** Pleasant or enjoyable to be around.
5. **Devoted:** Describing someone who is very loyal
6. **Eager:** Describing someone who is excited to do something.
7. **Friendly:** Describing someone who is kind and agreeable.
8. **Frivolous:** Describing someone who is carefree or unserious.
9. **Happy:** Describing someone that is pleasant.
10. **Insincere:** Describing someone that is not honest.
11. **Sad:** Describing someone who is showing unhappiness or sorrow.
12. **Shy:** Describing someone who is timid.
13. **Silly:** Describing someone who lacks common sense or judgment.
14. **Sincere:** Describing someone that is honest.
15. **Weak:** Describing someone who struggles with strength.

Quantity Adjectives

1. **All:** Describing the entirety of a set.
2. **Double:** Describing twice as many of something.
3. **Empty:** Lacking something entirely.
4. **Enough:** Something that is satisfactory.
5. **Few:** Describing some of a set.
6. **Full:** Something that is filled up to capacity.

7. **Great:** Having a large number of something.
8. **Little:** Something that is small or less.
9. **Lots of:** Describing something that is abundant.
10. **Most:** Having the majority of a set.
11. **Numerous:** Having many of something.
12. **Several:** Describing many of something.
13. **Sparse:** Something that is few and far between.
14. **Substantial:** Describing a significant amount of something.
15. **Whole:** Something that is complete.

Sense Adjectives

1. **Bland:** Something that is not very flavorful.
2. **Blurry:** Hard to see clearly.
3. **Brilliant:** Bright and colorful.
4. **Buzzing:** Having the appearance or quality of a vibrating sound.
5. **Cool:** Something that is neither warm nor cold to the touch.
6. **Faded:** Showing that the colors are starting to dull.
7. **Gloomy:** Dark and dreary.
8. **Hazy:** Unclear.
9. **Hushed:** Intentionally keeping something quiet.
10. **Limp:** Something that is loose and without resistance.
11. **Nauseating:** Something that is unpleasant and creates nausea.
12. **Odorless:** Something that doesn't have a smell.
13. **Scented:** Something that has some degree of scent.
14. **Scratchy:** Something that is rough and leads to abrasions.
15. **Screeching:** Something that is shrill and high pitched.

Size and Shape Adjectives

1. **Angular:** Something with sharp corners and lines.
2. **Big:** Large.
3. **Broad:** Something that is wide.
4. **Chunky:** Something that has considerable heft to it.
5. **Colossal:** Very large.
6. **Crooked:** Something that is not straight.
7. **Curved:** Something that gently bends.
8. **Deep:** Something that extends far beyond the surface.
9. **Flat:** Something that is without bumps or dents.
10. **Hollow:** Something that is empty inside.
11. **Massive:** Something that is majorly large.
12. **Measly:** Something that is small.
13. **Rounded:** Something that is curved.
14. **Scrawny:** Something that appears to be weak, skeletal, and thin.
15. **Small:** Something that is diminutive in size.

Time Adjectives

1. **Ancient:** Very old, relating to something that happened before modern times.
2. **Brief:** Very short in duration.
3. **Early:** Something that happened at the beginning of something.
4. **Late:** Something that happens toward the end of something or after it should have already occurred.
5. **Later:** Something that will happen in the future.
6. **Modern:** Something that is current or up to date.
7. **Old:** Something that happened long ago.

8. **Present:** Something that is current.
9. **Quick:** Something that didn't last long.
10. **Young:** Something that is not very old at all; it was born or created recently.

Chapter 6: Commonly Mistaken Words in English

Sometimes, some words sound a lot similar to another word that has a very different meaning. These are known as homophones, and they can be tricky if you are learning a new language. These words end up mistaken by many people, even native speakers. These are words that you need to know so that you can be certain that you are using the right one. We are going to look at several pairs of words that confuse many English speakers, and are likely to give you trouble as well.

Lose and Loose

Lose is a verb, while loose is a noun. They both sound quite alike, and many people mistake them. However, lose is to fail to win something while loose is something that is not tight.

Ex.

I lose every time I try to play that game!

This shirt is a bit too loose for me. I need a smaller size.

Resign and Re-Sign

These two are understandably mixed up, but they are two different words with a slightly different emphasis. Resign is pronounced more like reh-sine, while re-sign is re (like really) and sign. They are both verbs with very different meanings.

Resign is to give up on something, as in:

I resign from this job because I want to get a new one.

Re-sign is to sign something again.

I need to re-sign my lease so that the apartment complex knows I'll be here another year.

Advice and Advise

These two are a matter of a noun and a verb. Advice is the noun—when you advise someone, you give them advice. Advise, then, is the noun.

I advise you to heed my advice!

I am advising you that this is your best choice.

My advice still stands: You need to act now.

Affect and Effect

Affect, and effect is another matter of noun and verb. Affect is a verb most of the time, while effect is usually a noun. The best way to keep these straight is to try substituting the word "alter" and "result" to see which one fits better. If you can substitute in "alter," you can probably assume that affect is the word of choice. If you can substitute in result, effect is the right choice for you. For example:

My attempt to win affected everyone on my team.

The effect of my actions was felt by everyone.

Compliment and Complement

Compliment and complement are actually two distinctly different words that you will have to consider separately. You want to ensure that you do not mix these up. Compliments are nice—they are things that people say that are kind to the other person. Complements are things that tend to work well together.

Thanks for the compliment! I was so happy to hear you say that you like my dress.

These two colors are very complementary—they work well together!

Disinterested and Uninterested

Disinterested means impartial, while uninterested means bored or not wanting to get involved. As you can see, you can be engaged in something and disinterested—you are not going to be partial to any side of the argument at hand. However, you cannot be engaged and uninterested—if you are uninterested, you do not care to be involved in something.

The disinterested judge was able to make a fair verdict because he didn't have any ties to either side.

Fred was very uninterested in hearing what Allie had to say. She was always so boring!

Wary and Weary

Wary and weary may be close together when they are written out, but they are not the same words at all. Wary implies heavy caution about a subject while weary implies that you are exhausted.

I'm weary after a long day of hiking!

I was wary as I walked down the dark alley in the middle of the night.

Accept and Except

To accept something is to welcome or acknowledge it as true. Except, on the other hand, marks an exception to a rule—it shows that something is not true or is an outlier in the situation.

I accepted the gift graciously.

I liked all of the food except for the mashed potatoes.

Then and Than

Than and then are commonly mistaken as well. Than is used in comparisons while then is used in marking the passage of time. Effectively, when you use than, you are comparing two things together, such as saying that one is better than the other. In contract, if you are using then, you are talking about how you did one thing, then the next.

I was late to work, then got scolded by my boss.

I was earlier than I was the day before.

Their, There, and They're

These three words are all pronounced the same way, but they have very different meanings that have to be considered. Their is used to show possessiveness over something. There refers to a place. They're is a contraction that is used to combine they and are into one word.

Their dog is really cute!

There is a pizza on the table.

They're excited to eat pizza today!

Too, Two, and To

Too, two, and to are commonly mistaken because they all sound the same as well. However, you can note that they are still different. Too is used to say also. Two is a number, and to is used to imply motion or the infinitive of a verb.

I want to go, too!

He ate two pieces of cake.

I want to go to the store.

Chapter 7: Irregular Verbs

Irregular Verbs and Conjugations in English

Irregular verbs are those that do not follow the standard rules when they are conjugated. The most common is the verb, "to be," which conjugates:

I am

You are

He/she/it is

They are

These are verbs that you simply have to memorize the patterns and use them yourself. You will need to be well aware of how they conjugate as they do not have a pattern or rhyme or reason to them. There are all sorts of them in English, and they will be the most noticeable in the simple present and simple past tense. They will also typically alter the past participle as well, which is then used in the present perfect, past perfect, future perfect, passive, and past conditional forms.

Because irregular verbs are so prevalent, you will need to be wary of them. However, in terms of what they do and how to conjugate them, we are only going to go over the 10 most common in English. Be aware that there are several more as well that you will need to go through as well.

Common Irregular Verbs

To be

To be is commonly used in all sorts of different forms and is a verb that will impact several other tenses as well. You will see this playing out when you look at some of the more complex tenses as well, as you will discover soon. You can expect it to have the following forms:

Infinitive: be

Present tense: I am, he/she/it is, you/we/they are

Past tense: I, he/she/it was, we/you/they were

Past participle: Been

Present participle: Being

To have

To have is another common verb, but it is also irregular. It is conjugated in several different ways that do not match the normal patterns. You can expect this verb to conjugate with the following:

Infinitive: have

Present tense: I/you/we/they have, he/she/it has

Past tense: had

Past participle: had

Present participle: having

To say

We all say something from time to time—and the verb is quite irregular as well. From say, you somehow get said. The patterns that you can expect to see when you use this verb include:

Infinitive: say

Present tense: I/you/we/they say, he/she/it says

Past tense: said

Past participle: Said

Present participle: Saying

To do

To do is another common verb that you will need to have a good grasp over if you want to be able to speak well. Because this verb can be difficult, you will need to memorize the pattern.

Infinitive: do

Present tense: I/you/we/they do, he/she/it does

Past tense: did

Past participle: done

Present participle: doing

To know

To know is another verb that you will need to be mindful of in English. It is a very popularly used one, and it conjugates differently than the standard verbs that you are used to. You will expect to see patterns such as:

Infinitive: know

Present tense: I/you/we/they know, he/she/it knows

Past tense: knew

Past participle: known

Present participle: knowing

To get

When it comes to getting things, we do so in many ways. I get something while we all got something yesterday. This verb is irregular because of the letters in the middle change throughout the usage. Let's take a look at this conjugation as well.

Infinitive: get

Present tense: I/you/we/they get, he/she/it gets

Past tense: Got

Past participle: Gotten

Present participle: Getting

To see

When you are able to see things, you are able to do so in new ways. You get to see new things on a regular basis, and because of that, you need to be able to conjugate the word too! You didn't "seed" something yesterday—you *saw* it!

Infinitive: see

Present tense: I/you/we/they see, he/she/it sees

Past tense: saw

Past participle: seen

Present participle: seeing

To think

Thinking is something that you'll have to do if you want to conjugate this verb. Thankfully, the patterns aren't too bad! You can expect the following conjugations in English:

Infinitive: think

Present tense: I/you/we/they think, he/she/it thinks

Past tense: Thought

Past participle: Thought

Present participle: Thinking

To go

Go, despite being such a short word, also requires some extra conjugation as well. If you want to be able to conjugate go, you need to remember the following patterns:

Infinitive: go

Present tense: I/you/we/they go, he/she/it goes

Past tense: went

Past participle: gone

Present participle: going

To take

Taking things shouldn't be so complicated, and yet here we are! To take something is quite different than having taken it in the past. If you want to conjugate this word, you will need the following forms:

Infinitive: Take

Present tense: I/you/we/they take, he/she/it takes

Past tense: Took

Past participle: Taken

Present participle: Taking

Chapter 8: Compound Words

There are only so many words in the world, and because of that, we learn to create new ones by combining two others to create the meaning that we are looking for. We take two words and stick them together, and when we do that, we get a brand new word that has its own new definition.

For example, take the words sun and flower. When you smoosh them together, you get sunflower. It's not a sun—but it does look like one. We have all sorts of different words that exist in English that do this—they are there to ensure that we are able to get our meanings across in ways that are helpful to us. When you combine two words, you create what is known as a compound word. The types of words that you can end up with can vary greatly. Sometimes, the meaning makes sense. Sometimes, it might seem a little bit weird, but it works out. Learning to navigate through compound words is essential to be fluent in English, and the sooner that you can develop that fluency and understanding, the better.

Within this chapter, we are going to look at the three different kinds of compound words, how they are made, and then take a look at some of the most common compound words that you are likely to run into during your time studying and learning English.

The Types of Compound Words

Compound words are not all created equally—there are all sorts of different ones that exist, and you will need to be able to recognize them all at the end of the day if you want to ensure that your writing is up to par. While in spoken English, the form that you are using isn't as important, it does matter in written English: The spelling of the world is dependent upon the type of compound word that it is. When it comes to compound words, they will most likely be either closed compound words, open compound words, or hyphenated compound words.

Closed compounds

Closed compounds are compound words that are written as one word together. Both parts of the world come together to create just one word that is used. These are words such as newspaper, rainbow, catfish, and other words that involve two separate words that come together into one.

Open compounds

Open compounds are those that don't get completely combined, but they are still one particular noun or thing. These are concepts such as fishing pole, finishing line, pizza cutter, party favor, or other nouns that are built up of two other words that are paired together to create a new meaning.

Hyphenated compounds

Hyphenated compounds are those that are connected with a hyphen. These are quite simple to use but aren't as common as the others. They include words such as merry-go-round, will-o-wisp, or well-known.

Creating Compound Words

Creating compound words is simple—you just combine two words and get a new meaning. However, there are only so many that actually exist in English. You will have to know if the two words that you are combining are fair to pair together as one word, if they need to be together without being combined, or if you will need a hyphen to connect them together.

In spoken English, these really won't matter or influence what you are doing, but they are important to understand and recognize.

Commonly Used Compound Words

Now, let's go over a list of words that are commonly used:

- Baseball: A game in which a ball and bases are used
- Bookstore: A store that sells books
- Crosswalk: The point at which you are allowed to walk across the road
- Dance hall: A place reserved for dancing
- Dog trainer: Someone who trains dogs to behave
- Dragonfly: A kind of flying insect that has a long body and wings that looks vaguely like a dragon

- Fireworks: The art of working with explosives or fire in the air to create explosions that are aesthetically pleasing
- Fishbowl: The bowl that is used for a fish to live in on a table or counter
- Full moon: The moon when the entire face of it is visible
- Good-looking: Someone that looks good
- Groundhog: A type of animal that lives in the ground
- Headache: The feeling of pain or discomfort in the head
- Hush-hush: Something deemed a conspiratorial secret
- Ice cream: a frozen cream dessert
- In-laws: The family of one's spouse
- Jumping jacks: Exercises that involve jumping and clapping
- Landslide: The event in which the land is saturated with water and slips
- Laptop: A portable computer that is designed to sit atop one's lap for use.
- Lifejacket: A floatation device that is used to save people who accidentally fall in the water by keeping them at the top of the water
- Lighthouse: A building designed to shine a light so that ships know that there is land there at night
- Living room: The main room in a home that is used for get-togethers
- Mailman: A person that delivers the mail
- Mobile phone: The phones that we have with mobile service—they are not tied to lines physically
- Moonlight: The light that comes from the moon

- Mother-in-law: The mother of one's spouse
- Outer space: The universe outside of the Earth
- Party hat: A hat that is usually saved for parties
- Paycheck: A check designed to provide one's weekly pay
- Pizza cutter: A device designed to cut pizza easier than a knife would
- Rainbow: The display of colors that arch across the sky when it has been raining, and the sun is at just the right angle to reflect through the droplets
- Rainwater: The water created by a rainstorm
- Rattlesnake: A snake with a rattle on its tail
- Saucepan: A pan that is typically used with sauces
- Serving platter: A platter that is used to provide food at a meal
- Solar system: The planets surrounding the sun
- Soundproof: An area that is impervious to sound
- Tablespoon: A large spoon commonly used for eating
- Taxpayer: Someone who pays taxes
- Teaspoon: A small spoon that is commonly used for stirring drinks
- Well-known: something that everyone knows matter-of-factly

PART III

Chapter 1: Ricky Responsibility

Ricky Responsibility was a hero of responsibility. His number one mission in life was to teach children everywhere about the importance of responsibility.

Ricky Responsibility taught children to wash their clothes, their toes, and their nose. He taught children to put away their toys and to be kind to all the girls and boys. Ricky always wanted to see children be good and do the things they knew they should.

Whether it is learning right from wrong, or cleaning their rooms after a day so long, Ricky Responsibility wants to see every kid make the right choice.

Learning to take responsibility for yourself, and to fulfill your responsibilities in life is not always easy. Ricky Responsibility knows that, so he teaches his friends three important rules.

The first rule Ricky Responsibility teaches is the rule of *getting the job done*. No matter how hard it may be, you are the one to get the job done, and the job *must* get done! Whether it's helping your Mom buy groceries or helping your Dad mow the lawn, there is always something that needs to be done. Doing your part to get it done means the job is a lot easier for everyone!

The second rule Ricky Responsibility teaches is the rule of being thoughtful. Your actions always affect others, and you want your actions to help others, not hurt them. By being thoughtful, you make the world a wonderful place for everyone around you, so they can enjoy being around you, too!

The third rule Ricky Responsibility teaches is the rule of owning your actions. You must own all of the actions you take, whether they are good, bad, or a mistake. Since you have chosen them, they are your actions to own up to, and that is exactly what you should do. When you own the actions you take, you can fix your mistakes, learn right from wrong, and do better than you have ever done!

When you take responsibility for yourself, everyone cheers! You may even hear the cheers of Ricky Responsibility himself, as he cheers you on for becoming your best self!

Chapter 2: Hannah Learns About Hard Work

Working hard may not always seem fun, but it is an important way to get your work done. Hannah learned a great deal about hard work when her grandpa came over to help her dad build a new shed in the backyard. Hannah's mom needed a shed for her garden tools, and her dad wanted to keep his lawnmower in there, too. Hannah's dad even told her that once the shed was built, she could store her bike in the shed, too! She really wanted a place to store her bike that would be very special for herself.

When Hannah's grandpa got there, Hannah was determined to help build the shed so that they could build it as fast as possible. After all, the sooner the shed was built, the sooner Hannah would have a place for her bike!

First, Hannah helped her grandpa and dad collect the tools they needed to build the shed. They went to the hardware store and bought boards, nails, and a door for the shed. Then, they went home and unloaded the tools into the backyard so they could get ready to build the shed together.

When all of the tools were in the backyard, Hannah helped her grandpa and dad read the blueprint or the plans for how to build the shed. Then, they laid all of the wood out to show where each board would be hammered into place. Hannah helped her grandpa and dad carry the wood, lay it out, and then she helped them hold it in place so they could hammer the boards together.

Once most of the boards were in place, Hannah's dad even let her hammer some of them together! She fixed boards where they belonged, hammered nails into place, and made sure that she built the shed nice and sturdy so all of her mom's garden tools, her dad's lawnmower, and her bike would have somewhere to stay.

After all of the boards were in place, Hannah, her grandpa, and her dad cut a hole for the door and fixed the door into place, too. They tested it to make sure it worked by swinging the door open and closed. Hannah ran inside, closed the door, and then opened the door and popped back out. "Do you see me?!" She asked, giggling from behind the door. "We see you!" her dad and grandpa said, smiling back.

When they were all done, Hannah helped her mom put her garden tools in the new shed. Then, she helped her dad roll the lawnmower in and place it in the corner where it would stay from now on. Finally, Hannah rode her bike into the shed and set it up in its very own spot. She put her helmet on the handlebars and smiled, pleased with the new parking spot she had built for her bike with the help of her grandpa and her dad.

Chapter 3: Chester Gains His Confidence!

Chester could be very scared. Anytime he had to try something new, Chester would feel fear growing inside of him. He would worry about what he had to do, what others would be doing, and about what he did not know.

One day, Chester's mom signed him up for a field trip at school. He was going to be going to the aquarium with his friends! He knew it would be a lot of fun, but Chester could not help but feel scared. He worried about the bus ride there, all the new people, and all the new things he would see. Chester worried he would get lost, that all of the new people would overwhelm him, or that he would see a scary fish at the aquarium.

As they got on the bus, Chester's teacher noticed he was scared. "Are you ok?" His teacher asked. "No! I'm scared!" Chester said. "Why?" His teacher asked. "What if I don't like it? Or I see something scary? What if I get lost!" He said. "I understand, Chester. I would be scared, too, if I saw something scary or got lost. But you will not see anything scary, and you will not get lost. And I know you will like our trip to the aquarium!" His teacher said. "What if I don't?" Chester whined. "You will." His teacher said.

Chester climbed on the bus, still worried about how he felt. He walked all the way to the middle of the bus and sat down next to his friend Tomas. "What's wrong?" Tomas asked. "I'm scared," Chester said. "Why are you scared?" Tomas asked. "Because I've never been to the aquarium before!" Chester whined. "Me neither. I'm so excited!" Tomas said. Chester looked at Tomas, eyes wide with shock. "Really? You are excited?" Chester asked. "Yes! I want to see a big whale!" Tomas smiled. "Oh, that would be fun!" Chester agreed. "Yes! And I want to see the gift shop! I want to buy a shark! My mom gave me money." Tomas smiled. Chester thought about the money his mom gave him earlier that morning. "Well, that would be fun." Chester agreed.

Chester looked out the window as they drove to the aquarium. When he got there, Chester jumped out of his seat, feeling a little more excited. For a moment, he was scared by all of the new sights and people. Then, Chester remembered how Tomas said he was excited to see a whale and to buy a new shark. Chester wanted to do those things, too! He started to feel excited.

As Chester walked through the gates into the aquarium, he felt his confidence growing. He knew he was going to have fun with his friend Tomas! For the rest of the day, Chester practiced being confident. By the time they were leaving the aquarium, he was very sad because he was having so much fun!

Chester was surprised that being confident made him have so much more fun than he did when he was scared. Chester decided from then on that he would be confident about new experiences, even if he did feel a little scared sometimes.

Chapter 4: Carly Learns to Communicate

Carly was excited to start school with her friends. She had already been to preschool and kindergarten, so Carly knew what going back to school was like. She was excited about making a name tag, introducing herself to her teacher, and making new friends. She was especially excited about gym class because now Carly was old enough to play soccer with the other kids!

When she arrived at school on the first day, Carly noticed things were very different. This year, her friends were not sitting at circle tables with coloring pencils in the middle. Instead, they were sitting at small desks, all pointed to the front of the room, and they had no coloring pencils on them. In fact, they didn't have anything on them.

When class started, things were different. They did not stand in a circle and introduce themselves. Instead, they each stood next to their desk and said hello, said three things about themselves, then sat down. There was not much time for coloring because they had learning to do. They didn't even have a story circle on the first day. Things were very different from preschool and kindergarten.

At the end of the day, Carly was feeling sad and angry because the day did not go the way she wanted it to. Carly missed kindergarten. When her dad came to pick her up, instead of being kind, Carly was rude. She threw her bag in the car, jumped into her seat, kicked the seat in front of her, and ignored her dad. Carly's dad knew something was wrong, but he did not know *what* was wrong. Because he did not know what was wrong, Carly's dad could not help her. Carly stayed angry and had no one to help her feel better.

When they got home, Carly was still angry. She ran in the house, slammed the door behind her, and ran up to her room, and slammed that door, too. Now, Carly's dad was upset with her behavior. He wanted her to tell him what was wrong, but instead, she was not nice to him.

Carly's dad followed her up to her room, sat down at her desk, and asked her what was wrong. Finally, Carly told him. "School was not fun! I miss kindergarten!" she said. "Why?" her dad asked. "Because we sat with our friends and colored! Today, we did not sit with our friends or color! We did not even get storytime!" Carly cried. "I understand. That sounds very different from before." Her dad said, giving her a hug. "Thank you for telling me why you are so angry. Now, I know how to help you feel better. Before you did not tell me, so I did not know how to help you. How about we go color pictures together?" Her dad asked. "Yes please!" Carly said, hopping off the bed and running to color a picture with her dad, who happened to be one of her very best friends.

Chapter 5: Lester Learns a Lesson About Love

Lester was only six years old when he learned a lesson about love.

Lester knew that he loved his mom and dad, his little sister, and his dog, too. He also knew he loved his dinosaur toy and his bike, and his best friend, Jason.

When Lester thought about love, he thought about all the happy memories he had with his favorite people and toys. He thought about the time his friend came on a road trip with his family, and they brought their toy dinosaurs. He thought about the time he went fishing with his dad, and the time his mom taught him to bake muffins. Lester also thought about the time his best friend invited him for a sleepover, and they watched movies all night. When Lester thought about love, he thought about happy memories.

One day, Lester was tired after school. He sat down on the couch and relaxed, instead of putting his things away like his mom asked. Lester's mom asked him to clean up his things, but Lester did not listen. She asked one more time, then she turned off the TV and told him to go to his room.

"You do not love me!" Lester cried, running away. "That is not true." His mom said. "You do not love me! You are making me clean when I am tired!" He said again. "Lester, I am tired too, and these are not my things. I love you very much, but this is not my responsibility. You need to clean up your own belongings." His mom said. "I don't want to!" He cried. "I don't want to, either." His mom said. "You're mean! You make me do things I don't want to!" Lester said.

"Lester, I am tired, too. I still have my own things to do. How about this, would you like to clean the dishes, walk the dog, and mow the lawn so I can clean up your belongings?" His mom asked. Lester thought about it for a moment. "No." He said. "Exactly. Cleaning your things is your chore, and the other things are mine. I love you, but you need to respect me." His mom said. "I understand," Lester said as he went to clean up his things.

Lester thought about it as he cleaned up. He realized now that loving someone did not always mean happy memories and doing fun things together. Loving someone also meant respecting them and being kind to them. From then on, Lester was always respectful and kind to the people he loved.

Chapter 6: Felicia Spends Time With Family

Felicia loved spending time with her family. Most days, Felicia spent her family time with her parents and her two younger sisters. Sometimes, they would go to Felicia's grandparent's house, and they would spend time together with even more family. Felicia's aunt, uncles, and all of her cousins would come, too.

Felicia loved it when the whole family got together because it was always so much fun. She and her cousins would play in the backyard, her aunt and uncles would always have water gun fights with them, and her grandma and grandpa always made good food. Grandma made the best casseroles, and grandpa made the best pies.

Today, Felicia and her mom and dad and two sisters were going to be going over to her grandparent's house. She was so excited! She packed up all her things, put them in her bag, and got ready to leave. At exactly 11 in the morning, they packed up into the car and drove to grandma and grandpa's house. They got there shortly after 12.

Just as Felicia hoped, all of her family was there. She ran to say hello to her grandma, grandpa, aunt, two uncles, and nine cousins. Once they put their things down, Felicia and her cousins ran into the yard to play with their water guns. Felicia's aunt and uncles came out back and started playing, filling the water guns and spraying them all with the big soaker guns. Felicia's mom and dad joined, too, and at one point, her grandma and grandpa even started playing!

When it got later, Felicia's grandma brought out a fresh salad she had made.

The salad was so yummy. Then, Felicia's grandpa started barbecuing burgers. They ate their barbecued burgers and ate delicious pie for dessert. After they ate, her whole family went for a walk to a nearby park, and Felicia played on the playground with her sisters and cousins.

Later that night, Felicia and her family packed their things. Felicia, her mom and dad and both sisters all drove back home. On the way home, her parents asked if they had a good time. "I did! I love visiting family." Felicia smiled. "Me too!" her sisters said at the same time.

Chapter 7: Sean Gets Sick

Sean was sitting in his desk at school when, suddenly, he started feeling unwell. Sean felt hot, and his stomach was churning. He could feel himself getting more tired, so he laid his head down on his desk. "Are you ok, Sean?" his teacher asked. "No, I feel sick!" Sean said. "Oh no! We should call your parents. It is important to go home and relax when you are sick." His teacher said. "But I don't want to go home! I want to play with my friends!" Sean said. "I know. You can come back when you are feeling better. Your parents will come get you now." Sean's teacher said.

Sean really wanted to stay with his friends but agreed that it was important to get well first.

Sean's dad picked him up from school and brought him home. When they got home, Sean's dad helped him lie in bed and relax so he could start to feel better. "I don't want to relax; I want to play!" Sean whined. "I know, Sean. But you have to relax when you are sick. It helps you feel better when you have been sick." His dad said. "Will I feel better soon?" Sean asked. "Yes."

His dad said.

Sean laid in bed. His head felt warm, his nose felt stuffed, and his belly felt sick. Every time he rolled over, he winced as the pain got worse before it got better. After a while of just lying there, Sean finally fell asleep.

When he fell asleep, Sean dreamed about being at school with his friends. He dreamt about playing with the push cars, swinging on the swings, and going down the slide. Sean dreamt about having lunch with his friends, learning about the alphabet, and coloring in his favorite coloring book. He dreamt about everything he loved, which was many things because Sean really loved going to school.

Eventually, Sean woke up from his nap. When he did, his dad and mom were in the room with him. "How are you feeling?" his mom asked, resting the back of her hand on Sean's forehead. "Ok," Sean said. The cool touch of his mom's hand felt good against his forehead, which felt warm because of the fever he had from his sickness. "You still feel warm." She frowned. "I know." He sighed.

Sean's dad brought him a cup of water. Then, his mom brought him some chicken noodle soup. Sean drank the water and ate the soup, then laid back down against his pillow. Although he was still feeling sick, Sean started to feel some relief from his symptoms.

When his mom and dad left the room, Sean laid back down and rested his head against his pillow. Once again, he slept. This time, Sean dreamt about watching TV, climbing trees, and playing with his dog, Pal. Sean loved dreaming about wonderful things that made him happy.

It wasn't until the next morning when Sean woke up. His sickness had made him so tired that he slept all the way through dinner, and through the entire night! By morning, Sean was starting to feel much better. His fever was gone, his nose was clear, and his belly was almost all better.

"How are you feeling this morning?" His dad asked while his mom prepared their lunches. "A lot better, but my belly still hurts," Sean responded. "Do you feel good enough to go to school?" His dad asked. "No, but this time I will not be sad about it because I know how important it is to take care of myself. Tomorrow, I will be feeling completely better. I'm sure of it!" Sean said. "Sounds good." His mom smiled.

Sean spent the rest of the day lying in bed, working on feeling better. As the day went on, his tummy started to feel better. By the next morning, Sean was feeling completely better and ready to go back to school. So, he did! When he got there, he was so happy to be with his friends again, and to know that he had taken such good care of himself that he had plenty of energy to push cars, play on the swings, and go down the slides with his friends. It was a good day!

Chapter 8: Melissa Makes a New Friend

Melissa always played with her friends Kayla and Beth. Kayla and Beth lived on the other side of town, but their moms were friends, so they always got together to do fun things. When it was time for school to start, Melissa got nervous. Kayla and Beth would be going to the same school, but Melissa would be going to a different school where she knew no one.

The day before school started, Melissa's mom found her in her room crying. "What is the matter?" Her mom asked. "I will not have any friends at school. I do not want to go!" Melissa cried, worried that school would be scary with no friends. "That is why you are going to school to make new friends." Her mom smiled. "I don't want new friends. I like Kayla and Beth!" Melissa pouted. "Kayla and Beth are wonderful friends. It is good to have many friends, though, Melissa." Her mom said, hugging her. "I don't want many friends." Melissa kept crying. Melissa's mom hugged her close and thought about what to say.

"When I first started school, I was afraid, too." Her mom said. "You were?" Melissa asked. "Oh, yes! I worried no one would like me, and I would have no one to play with. I did not have friends like Kayla and Beth; either, I was all by myself." Her mom said. "That is said," Melissa said, crying still. "It was, but I made many wonderful friends at school. I did not believe my mom when she said I would, but I did! In fact, that is how I met Kayla and Beth's mom, and now we are still friends!" Her mom said. "Really?" Melissa asked, her eyes growing wide. "Really." Her mom smiled. "If you did not go to school, you would not have met her?" Melissa asked. "No." Her mom replied.

Melissa stopped and thought for a while. She watched the clouds go by as she thought about what school would be like. She wondered who she would meet, what they would be like, and if she would like any of them. Melissa wondered if she would have fun and if school wouldn't be so bad after all. Then, she wondered about what Kayla and Beth were going to do on their first day of school. She thought about how they, too, would be going into new classrooms, making new friends, and having fun. Melissa thought that if Kayla and Beth could do it, surely she could do it, too.

The next day, Melissa got up and got ready for school. She got dressed, brushed her teeth and her hair, ate breakfast, and laced up her shoes the way her dad had taught her. When the time was right, she grabbed her backpack and walked to the car with her mom. On the way to school, Melissa quietly thought about what the first day would be like. "Are you excited?" Her mom asked when they were almost there. "Yes." Melissa said, folding her hands in her lap. "Will you make new friends?" Her mom asked. "Yes." Melissa said, wondering if that was true.

When she arrived at school, Melissa felt afraid, but she knew that her friends would not want her to be scared. So, she bravely went inside and started getting to know new people. She started by introducing herself to her teacher. Then, she introduced herself to the people sitting near her. When class started, her teacher had everyone sit in a circle, and they all introduced themselves to each other. Melissa thought two of the girls in her class might make for wonderful friends. Their names were Ashley and Shupe.

At recess, Melissa introduced herself to Ashley and Shupe. The three of them got along really well and spent the entire time playing tag and talking about how excited they were for school to be starting. By the time recess was over, Melissa knew she had made two wonderful new friends.

When school ended, Melissa's mom picked her up. On the way home, her mom asked, "So, did you make any new friends?" "I did!" Melissa smiled. "Oh? Who are they?" Her mom asked. "Ashley and Shupe. They are in my class! We played tag at recess. I am excited to see them again tomorrow." Melissa said. "That is wonderful. I knew you would make friends! All you had to do was be brave, and try your best, and it worked!" Her mom smiled. "That's right!" Melissa smiled back.

Every day for the rest of the year, Melissa enjoyed playing with her friends Ashley and Shupe, and she also enjoyed playing with her friends Kayla and Beth. On her birthday, her mom even invited them all over, and they all played together and had great fun. Melissa realized she loved making friends and hoped she would make even more the next school year.

Chapter 9: Austin Learns to Care for Animals

Austin was six years old when his parents bought him his very own puppy. Radar, the brown Labrador retriever, was a friendly little fluffy puppy. He loved to lick hands, do tricks for treats, and go for walks with Austin and his parents. Although it was fun to get a new puppy, Austin realized they came with a lot of responsibility. That meant that Austin had to do a lot of work to take care of his little puppy, Radar!

Every morning, Austin had to clean the food and water dishes and give Radar fresh food and water. He would then take Radar into the backyard so the puppy could go to the bathroom. Once they came inside, Austin would put Radar's harness on, attach his leash, and get ready to take his dog for a walk. Austin's mom or dad would always help him, as walking around the block by yourself when you are only six years old is not always the safest thing to do. For Austin, it felt like a fun way to spend time with his parents before the day got started.

Once they got home, Austin made sure Radar had plenty of food, water, and toys to keep him going through the afternoon. He also made sure to shut the door to all of the bedrooms, as Radar was just a puppy, and sometimes he would go in there and chew things that he was not supposed to be chewing. When he was ready to go, Austin would give Radar a big hug and leave for school.

When Austin got home, there were still plenty of chores to do so that he could take care of Radar! He would refill his food and water, and once again put a harness and leash on Radar so they could take him for his afternoon walk. If Radar went to the bathroom on that walk, Austin would have to pick it up with a bag so he could put it in the garbage.

After they got home, Austin would take Radar in the backyard and throw a ball for him to help Radar get all of his energy out. Then, he would take out the training treats and teach Radar new tricks. Austin taught Radar how to sit, lie down, jump, bark on command, and shake a paw. Every day, they would practice a new trick, so Radar could learn something cool and interesting.

Before bed, Austin would have to play with Radar again to make sure Radar was good and tired, so he would sleep through the night. He would throw the ball for him, teach him more tricks, and sometimes take him for another walk if his dad was home from work. Then, he would tuck Radar in so he could go to sleep in his very own bed.

Whenever Radar got sick, Austin would have to take Radar to the vet. He also had to take Radar to the vet for his puppy checkups and annual checkups, as well as to get him his shots. Taking proper care of his dog was an important way to make sure his friend was always happy, healthy, and well cared for.

Austin loved having a dog, but having his very own dog taught him that puppies were a lot of work! Still, Austin knew that his best friend was worth it, and was happy that his parents let him have his new best friend. For the rest of their lives together, Austin always cherished and cared for Radar the very best he could, which is why Radar lived a long, happy, and healthy life.

Chapter 10: Chelsea Discovers Consistency

Chelsea really wanted to be the best scorer on the basket team, but no matter how hard she tried, it always seemed like she couldn't do it. Every Thursday, Chelsea would practice with her teammates, yet no matter how hard she tried, she could barely score one basket. Eventually, Chelsea got upset and wanted to quit playing basketball.

"You can't quit playing!" Her friends argued. "I have to; I'm no good." She sighed.

When her coach heard she wanted to quit, she tried to help Chelsea feel better about her ability to play. "Chelsea, I heard you want to quit. Before you do, I want you to try one thing for me. When you go home after school every day, try scoring baskets at home. See how well you do!" Her coach said. "But how will that make me any better?" Chelsea asked. "You will see. If I'm wrong, I will let you quit." Her coach smiled.

Every day after school, Chelsea went home and practiced playing basketball.

For the first week, Chelsea was terrible at it. She saw no improvement. In fact, she may have gotten worse because she was not used to the hoop she had at home.

After that week, though, Chelsea got better.

At first, she only got a little better.

Over time, she was scoring every single basket.

Chelsea showed up at school the following week, ready to show off her new skills. Her teammates were shocked to see her improvement, but her coach was not.

"I knew you could do it!" Her coach smiled.

"Thank you, coach!" Chelsea said, scoring another basket.

"You see, consistency really does pay off." Coach said.

"What does it mean to be consistent?" Chelsea asked.

"It means you keep doing it over and over again until you get the results you want." Her coach taught her.

"I love consistency!" Chelsea cheered, scoring yet another basket. Now, she had what it took to be the best scorer on the team.

Chapter 11: Barney Becomes Brave

Barney was afraid of bees. He was so afraid of bees that anytime he saw them; he would scream and run in the opposite direction.

"I don't like bees!" he would yell, running away.

One day, Barney's dad wanted to show him that bees were not scary. He also wanted to show Barney how to be brave around his fears.

Barney's dad took him outside, and together they found a bee. Right before Barney screamed and ran away, Barney's dad said, "Look! I want to show you something cool!" So, Barney looked.

At first, Barney was scared. Then, he saw his dad take the bee and bring it into the house. Barney was surprised. Barney's dad put the bee in a little cup and told him to look at it, so he did. As he looked in, Barney saw the little fuzzy bee crawling around inside the cup. At first, he thought the bee looked scary. As he kept watching, though, the bee kept moving around, and Barney started to think that the bee looked cute.

After a few minutes, Barney's dad let the bee out of the cup and asked Barney to carry it back out to the garden. Barney was scared and did not want to, but his dad assured him he would be okay because male bumblebees do not bite, and this was a male bumblebee. Finally, Barney agreed and let the little bee crawl on his finger. Then, he carefully walked outside and put the bee on a flower in the garden.

"Was that so bad?" his dad asked.

"No!" Barney smiled, looking at the bee.

"Well done for being brave, Son!" His dad cheered, high fiving Barney.

Chapter 12: Talia Learns About Team Work

Talia was a good, strong worker. She always finished her homework on time, could score a goal at any sport, and was the best on her team no matter what game she played. There was only one problem: Talia was bad at sharing.

When they played team sports, Talia never shared the ball with anyone else. She would hog the ball and avoid passing it to anyone else, hoarding all of the shots for herself. When coach called on everyone to pick their positions, Talia would pick offense every time so she could be the one leading the team to scores. Talia loved being in control and guiding her team to success.

In class, group projects never went well, either. Talia would not let anyone else do any work, and would instead do everything herself. Talia would do the research, write everything down, create the projects, and hand them in. When it came time to grade everything, Talia would tell the teachers that she did all the work because her teammates refused to help. This was a lie, but the teachers did not know better.

One day, Talia told her teacher this very lie, and her group member spoke up.

"That is not true!" She said.

"Yes it is!" Talia said.

"No! We tried to help, but you did not let us." Her classmate insisted.

"Is this true?" The teacher asked.

"No!" Talia argued.

"Yes." All her group members said.

"Talia, that is not nice. You have to share the responsibility, that is the point of group projects. You need to learn to work together with others." Her teacher said.

The next day, Talia's teacher made her do another group project. This time, her teacher showed her how to work with a team. Talia's teacher showed her how to let other's research, write, and build the project with her. At first, Talia did not like sharing. Soon, she realized it was much easier when she had her friends helping her, so she welcomed the help of her team members.

Once Talia learned to work as a team member, she wanted to work as a team on *everything*. With homework, she happily let her group members help her. When she was on the sports field, she shared the ball and offered her team a chance to play. Even at home Talia was a better team player, as she let her siblings take part in the things they were doing together.

Talia realized that being a team player was so fun because they got way more done, and they all won. By the end, Talia *loved* teamwork!

PART IV

1 POEMS ABOUT GOOD FEELINGS

Happy

I went to see my friend,
His name was Carter Blue.
He liked to play with blocks,
And I kind of like them, too.

We play all day together,
Smiles ear to ear,
And when we play, I have to say,
I could stay all year.

Carter is my buddy,
We even share our snack.
Sometimes I take his toy,
But I always give it back.

We sit and watch a movie,
Or maybe play a game,
But sometimes we just sit,
And I feel good, just the same.

On days when I get bored,
It's Carter that I call,
He'll always make me feel good,
We always have a ball.

And that's what I call happy,
Warm and safe and free,
That's how I feel with Carter,
And happy works for me.

Excited

Today is the day that I get to go
Up on the ride where just big kids go.

It goes super high up to the sky
And now I could cry, "It's my turn, oh my!"

I wait in the line that goes all around.
I stand on my toes, don't want to touch ground.

"I see it, I see it! It's here, yes it is!"
I am jumping and clapping, like soda I fizz.

I know it is close now, coming so quick.
"It's me, it's me! It's me you should pick!"

They wave me to go now, my waiting is done,
I climb on the ride, ready for fun!

"You must be excited," my mom says to me.
Excited is right, but I just say, "Weeeee!"

Calm

I sit on the sofa with my good friend Bear,
I know he's not real, but I do not care.

He is so fuzzy, brown and kind.
He cannot talk, but I do not mind.

Next I find blanket, pull it up close,
This is the part that I like the most.

I do not move, I do not wiggle,
I do not play, I do not giggle.

This is the time when I can sit still,
You think that I can't, but I know I will.

My dad says I'm calm, and that could be right,
But I do not care, as I sit here all night.

Silly

Come with me, you should see,
Watch me go so crazy!
Going up, going down,
Turning flips like a clown!

Watch this skip,
Watch this hop,
Watch me go,
I can't stop!

Then a joke, then a poke,
Then a clap and a tap,
Then I roll on the floor,
Laugh until I am sore.

Do you want to see more?
Oh, I have much more!

Did you see, see my face?
Now let's go have a race!
I zoom here, I zoom there,
Come and catch me, if you dare!

Do a dance, next I prance,
Do a shake, eat some cake.
Am I done? No way, pal!
I am one silly gal.

Surprised

School is now over,
It's finally done,
And all I want now,
Is some fun in the sun.

I walk to the bus,
I hop up the step,
"Hey, good day, Fred?"
And I say back, "Yep!"

I get to my door,
And open it slow,
See, it's my birthday,
You know how birthdays go!

Soon I'll have gifts,
And plenty of food,
Maybe a cake?
I'm in the mood!

But no one is home,
The lights are not on,

Where is my family?
Could they be gone?

I walk room to room,
Not sure what to do,
When all of a sudden,
I hear, "Yoohoo!"

The lights now flash on,
And I see everyone,
They're yelling "Surprise!"
And I say, "Time for fun!"

2 POEMS ABOUT THE PLAYGROUND

Swings

I am sitting,
Sitting on the swing,
And as I get ready,
I start to sing.

"Here we go up,
Up to the sky,
And if we push hard,
We can go high!"

"I push my legs up,
I push my legs down,
I want to see clouds,
Not see the ground."

I start to swing faster,
Kicking so quick,
Soon I'll be there,

Lickety-split!

I want to touch blue,
Want to go soar,
Want to get there,
Want to see more.

If I go high,
Then I can be,
Just like a bird,
Happy and free.

I sing it again,
And I sing it so loud,
This time I know,
I will reach a cloud.

Slides

I climb up the rungs,
Filling my lungs,
This will be great!
I cannot wait!

I'm at the top,
No need to stop,
Take a look down,
Then kind of frown.

It's kind of high…
I don't want to cry…
My friends will all see…
I could hurt my knee…

I look to the left,
No one.
I look to the right,
No one.

I take a big step,
My mind is now set,

I can do this,
I will not miss.

Now I will sit,
And slowly I tip,
Should I let go?
Slide high to low?

I do it, too late!
And hey, this is great!
I *can* take the slide!
It is one great ride!

Monkey Bars

Grab this one,
Grab that one,
Keep going,
Must have fun.

Grab again,
Grab both hands,
Don't give up,
I must land.

Grab the bar,
Grab so far,
I might fall,
Fall so far.

Grab with care,
Grab the air,
Down I go,
It's not fair!

Scrape my knee,
Scratch my face,

Cry some tears,
Hate this place!

Then my mom,
Nice and calm,
Comes to say,
"Hey, come on!"

"We all fall,
Yes, yes all,
It's okay,
You are small."

"It takes time,
You will find,
You can try,
Make up your mind."

"You can play,
That's okay,
You will do it,
Do it someday."

I sit and sigh,

"I guess I'll try…"

I go across!

"I can!" I cry.

Seesaw

When you go up,
I go down,
When you go high,
I touch the ground.

It's back and forth,
It's you and me,
The two of us,
Are so happy.

I push up hard,
You go down fast,
I laugh a lot,
I hope it lasts!

We can't stop now,
It's fun and free,
We love this game,
We're so happy.

We want to play,
A new fun game,

It looks like here,
But not the same.

We're on a ship!
The sea is high,
We can't fall off,
You and I.

We rock about,
Both high and low,
But overboard,
We cannot go.

So hold on tight,
The ship will rise,
The waves will crash,
The sun will rise.

And now the waves,
Begin to slow,
We're safe home now,
No need to row.

We did so well,

We did it, friend.

Now let's hop off,

That's the end!

Jump Rope

Watch me jump this rope,
Think I'll fall? Nope!

I can rock this thing.
Move my legs like wings.

They flap down and up,
I never mess it up.

The rope goes round and round,
Slapping on the ground.

I count and count some more,
I try to keep my score.

I cannot keep going,
I show no sign of slowing.

Jumping is my jam
Grab that rope and BAM!

This girl cannot be stopped,

My score cannot be topped!

This rope and I will win,
I wear a nice big grin.

Jumping is my game,
Sandra is my name.

Hey, just watch my feet.
I cannot be beat.

Want to try it now?
Beat me? I don't know how!

3 POEMS ABOUT FRIENDSHIP

Friend

So I like you,
And you like me,
We like to play,
As you can see.

We like robots,
And big toy cars,
We like our blocks,
And dinosaurs.

And if you cry,
I will come,
To see what's wrong,
Make sure it's done.

And if I fall,
I know you'll be,
Right there real soon,

You will help me.

You make me laugh.
You make me smile.
You make me happy,
For a long while.

So that's a friend,
Someone who's there,
They always come,
They show they care.

Sometimes you fight,
Sometimes you cry,
But it will stop,
When they come by.

Good friends you keep,
Good friends stay near,
Good friends are special,
Good friends are dear.

Making New Friends

I really want a friend,
A playing pal for me,
I really want a friend,
Is it so hard to see?

But how do I get started?
How do I find someone?
Do I shout, "Be my friend!"
Or poke them and then run?

No, that isn't right,
I can't find nobody.
I am stuck alone,
Bored without a buddy.

Then my dad comes by,
He says, "What's got you sad?"
I don't know what to say…
"I've got no friends, it's bad!"

He says, "Now just you wait,
That cannot be true,

Everyone would want,
An awesome friend like you."

He says, "Let's fix this now,
I think I've got a plan,
You will make a friend,
You'll do it, yes you can!"

"First, you walk up close,
But not too close, you see,
And then you say, 'Hello!'
And they may smile, maybe."

"And if they smile at you,
You can say some more,
Like, 'Do you want to play?'
That's what this ball is for."

"Take this ball with you,
And squeeze it nice and tight,
You can squeeze so hard,
Squeeze with all your might."

"Making friends is scary,

Making friends is tough,
But when you squeeze that ball,
Remember, you're great stuff."

"If they will be your friend,
I'll be pumped for you,
And if they say no thanks,
You'll know what to do."

"You can come find me,
We will take a walk,
I'm a friend, you see,
And we can always talk."

Talk Time

"Hey!"
"Hello!"
"Ready?"
"Let's go!"

It's play time with Charlotte,
Play time again,
Time to see Charlotte!
I do a quick spin.

Charlotte is funny,
Charlotte is cool,
Charlotte likes baseball,
Crayons, and pools.

Then I see Charlotte,
And it's kind of weird…
I can't find my words!
It's just like I feared!

I want my friend,
To see I'm so chill,

I am the coolest,
But I just stand still…

How do I talk?
How do I walk?
How do I speak?
Can I just squeak?

Then Charlotte says,
"Um…should we play?"
And I can say, "Yes!"
She saved the day!

Good or Bad?

I have a friend,
They are so great,
Well, I think they are…
But then again…wait…

Does a good friend
Ask you to cheat?
Do they throw food
They don't want to eat?

Do they make sounds
During calm time?
Tell you it's apple
When really it's lime?

I just don't know,
This is not right,
A good friend is kind,
A friend does what's right.

I have a friend,
They are so great,

Well, I think they are…
But then again…wait…

Does a good friend
Always take turns?
Bring you a band aid
If you have burns?

Does a good friend
Share things with you?
Tell you great stories,
Tell you what's true?

That's a good friend,
Now I can see,
Because a good friend
Will look out for me.

Saying Goodbye

It's moving day,
But somehow I'm sad.
I should feel happy,
But I just feel bad.

Our new house is big,
Our new house is fun,
I like my room,
But I don't want to come.

Lily won't be there.
Lily must stay.
Lily's my friend,
But we cannot play.

She will stay here,
I will move on,
I cannot do it,
She will be gone.

It is not fair,
It is not nice,

I'd rather get sick,
I'd rather have lice.

She is my best friend,
Really, the best,
Not like my other friends,
Not like the rest.

We pull away,
The truck is now going,
I start to wave,
But I am crowing.

"What about Lily?
What will I do?"
Then my mom says,
"You can start new."

Old friends are great,
Old friends are true,
But new friends can come,
New, just for you."

4 POEMS ABOUT FUNKY FEELINGS

Anxiety

Today is the big game,
Today they chant my name.

It is all up to us,
We cannot cry or fuss.

I must help us win,
I must lift my chin.

"Do it!" they all say,
"Do it! Go and play!"

But what if I cannot?
What if I freeze and stop?

What if I cannot score?
What if they ask for more?

Will I be called so cool,
Or will I be a fool?

I take a breath so deep,
I close my eyes, don't peep.

This is too much for me,
Why can't they let me be?

I'm jumpy, worried, mad,
And maybe a little sad.

This is anxiety,
It lives inside of me.

It makes me doubt myself,
Want to hide up on a shelf.

But I will work, not quit,
Someday I'll conquer it.

Embarrassment

It's show time,
Show off time,
It's my line…
Oh no…mine!

It's too late,
I just hate,
That I choke,
My voice broke.

They all see,
I'm stuck, me,
And I freeze,
Don't even sneeze.

They all stare,
They all care,
Their smiles show,
The whispers grow.

I messed it up!
I've given up!

I cannot do it,
Cannot get through it!

Don't look at me,
Just let me be.
Just make it stop
So I can plop.

I want to sit,
Sit and forget,
My face turns red,
I want my bed.

Then I could hide,
Go deep inside,
All warm and safe,
Far from the hate.

Mistakes can happen,
They keep on coming,
But you get up,
Dust off, get tough.

Mistakes are fine,

Forget the line.
And soon you'll find,
They don't really mind.

Shyness

It's school today,
I have to go.

It's school today,
But I won't show.

It's school today,
But I will hide.

It's school today,
But I'm inside.

At home,
It's quiet,
No one to joke.

At home,
It's nice,
No one to poke.

At home,
It's safe,

No one to hurt me.

At home,
It's fun,
No one to leave me.

But school has kids,
And I like kids.

But school has friends,
And I want friends.

But school has toys,
And I like toys.

But school has recess,
And I want recess.

I'm sorry,
I don't talk,
But I can walk.

I'm sorry,
I don't run,

But I still like fun.

I'm sorry,

I'm still shy,

But friends come, let's say hi!

Stress

The test is coming soon,
The teacher says at noon.

I tried and tried to study,
I even called my buddy.

I stayed up late last night,
Got all the answers right.

And then I did my chores,
But think about high scores.

It's time to go do this,
There's nothing I can miss.

I must go here, go there,
I cannot stop to stare.

I must do everything,
No time to top and sing.

I must get it done,

Before the bell has rung.

It's time to take the test,
I think and try my best.

Now off to get haircut.
Try again to cheer up.

There's just too much to do,
But I have to make it through.

Jealousy

You got the biggest toy,
I guess that it's okay.
But it belonged to me,
Just the other day.

You should not have it now,
It's really not for you,
You should hand it over,
You should, shouldn't you?

You see, I really want it,
I know that we should share,
But I like it and I saw it,
But take it, I don't care…

But the toy, it was for me,
It was my special treat,
And it's you who has it now,
I guess you got me beat.

Why should you get to hold it?
It's really not that great.

You don't really want it,
You should really wait.

Why did you take my toy?
It should be mine to keep.
We had a lot of fun,
It honks and turns and beeps.

Alright, I guess it's your now,
I guess I'll just move on.
But I'll still want my toy,
Even when it's gone.

5 POEMS ABOUT PARENTS

Parents

They're sometimes nice,
Sometimes sweet,
Sometimes scary,
Sometimes neat.

I call them parents,
They seems to like it.
They call me "kiddo"
And I don't mind it.

They're sort of silly,
I like their smiles,
They do my laundry,
Make big piles.

I like their food,
Except the veggies,
They make my lunch,

In little baggies.

But there is more,
That makes them great,
So much to share,
I cannot wait.

They give big hugs,
They always mean it,
When I call home,
They know they're needed.

They gives their love,
Like they give food,
There's lots of it,
In every mood.

I'm sad,
They're there.
I'm bad,
They're there.

The best part of parents,
They're always there.

Not Inside the House!

I want to learn to ski.
Not inside the house!

I want to play football.
Not inside the house!

I want to waterslide.
Not inside the house!

I want to swing my bat.
Not inside the house!

I want to make mud pies.
Not inside the house!

I want to run around.
Not inside the house!

So many rules for me,
All inside the house.

There is no fun for me,

Not inside the house.

But skiing is on snow…
Not inside the house.

But football is on fields…
Not inside the house.

But waterslides are outside…
Not inside the house.

But bats are for baseball,
Not inside the house.

But mud pies are from dirt…
Not inside the house.

But running should go far…
Not stuck inside the house.
Because I Said So

My parents looked at me
And said just four short words.

"Because I said so!"
Those words could not be worse.

What do they even mean?
Does anybody know?

"Because I said so!"
Are you sure, though?

I have to ask you, "Why?"
I guess you have to say it.

"Because I said so!"
Is one way you can say it.

I guess I just don't see,
I guess I don't know how.

If I ask you why again,
Will you have a cow?

What do those four words mean?
Why do you say it so?

You take a big breath now,
I turn and start to go.

And then you say, "I love you.
And you should have the best."

"Sometimes I don't know why,
And so I say because."

"But all the things I say,
They come from all my love."

Time Out

They said it,
They said time out,
They said it,
And now I pout.

I hate time out,
It stinks.
I stand there,
Stand and think.

To stand here,
Is a bore.
To stand here,
Is a chore.

They time it,
Every time.
They make me stand,
On a line.

Why do I stand?
I ask.

They say,
Stay on task.

What's a task?
I'd like to know.
But it's time out,
They go.

I guess I'll stand,
Okay.
I'll stand,
I cannot play.

And then I start to think.
Why did they send me here?
And then I hear a whisper,
Right inside my ear.

I did something bad,
And I need to fix it.
Time out is my time,
To think and not to miss it.

Do This, Do That

You said I should study,
You said I should eat,
You said I should sleep,
You said wash your feet.

But why should I study?
And eat?
And sleep?
Why do I care
If my feet kind of stink?

You said I should wake up,
You said I should plan,
You said I should clean up,
You said give a hand.

But why should I wake up?
And plan?
And clean up?
Why do I care
If the room's messed up?

And then you talk back,
And now I can see.
You telling me to,
Is caring for me.

If I don't study,
And eat,
And sleep,
If I don't wake up,
And plan,
And clean up,

Life will be hard,
Life will be crazy,
When you say "Do this!"
You're thinking of me.

6 POEMS ABOUT SIBLINGS

Brothers and Sisters

I want to be alone,
But you are always there.

You like to tickle me,
Put old gum in my hair.

You never let me see,
You always get there first.

You get the coolest stuff,
You really are the worst.

Your door is always shut,
Sometimes it makes me scream.

You always shut me out,
It's really kind of mean.

But when the door is open,
When we sit and talk,
It's really kind of nice,
We play and laugh and walk.

When parents make us crazy,
And school is just so hard,
You grab my hand and say,
"Let's go play in the yard."

When the day is done,
And you are still by me,
I look at you and think,
"This is the way to be."

It's MY Room!

I said,
DON'T come in.

I said,
DON'T touch.

I said,
DON'T visit.

Did I ask too much?

You can be…
Boring.

You can be…
A bug.

You can be…
Loud.

I said DON'T pull the plug!

You don't seem to get it.

You really must not see.

I don't want you in here.

DON'T spend time with me.

How come you do not know?

And why DON'T you just go?

I guess,
You can be cute.

I guess,
You can be sweet.

I guess,
You can be funny.

I guess,
You're kind of neat.

Okay, you can come in.

Okay, you can touch.

Okay, you can visit.

You DON'T ask too much.

Oh, Brother

You're such a bother, brother.
You scream and kick and cry.

You're such a bother brother,
I hang my head and sigh.

You're such a bother, brother,
You never can sit still.

You're such a bother, brother,
You sound so loud and shrill.

You're such a bother, brother,
You poke me way too much.

You're such a bother, brother,
You make me want to punch.

But then you say my name.
Oh, brother.

Then we play a game.

Oh, brother.

You giggle when I tickle,
Oh, brother.

You even share your pickle,
Oh, brother.

You give hug me big each day,
Oh brother.

I'm so glad you'll stay,
Oh, brother.

Tips for Sisters

When you have a sister,
It can be a lot.

She may take all the candy,
She may bang on a pot.

When you have a sister,
You can get real mad.

She may break your toy,
Or the doll you had.

When you have a sister,
She may get the time.

Parents can forget you,
Just like a lost dime.

When you have a sister,
It can be so cool.

She may say, "Hello!"

In the hall at school.

When you have a sister,
You can get real sad.

But she will come to save you,
Take away the bad.

When you have a sister,
Your parents may just see.

It's nice to have a sister,
Someone who will love me.

Siblings At School

You see your sister,
See your brother,
They're walking down the hall.

You say, "Hi!"
They walk by,
Like you're not real at all.

They are older,
You are younger,
They don't want to see.

You don't get it,
You are sad,
"Why don't they talk to me?"

They are cool,
You are not,
Guess it's just the rule.

You say nothing,
They keep walking,

No fun times at school.

Kids are mean,
Call you names,
You don't know what to do.

You start crying,
It's not fair,
But then they come to you.

You see your sister,
See your brother,
And they say, "What's wrong?"

They take your hand,
You both stand,
And then you walk along.

7 POEMS ABOUT BAD FEELINGS

Anger

You took it,
I know it,
And it's not okay.

You broke it,
I know it,
I'll get you today.

You lost it,
I know it,
And now you will pay.

You did it,
I know it,
I'll not let you stay.

I'm hot,
I'm panting,

I'm red,
I'm clenching.

You hurt me,
I know it,
And you have to go.

You hit me,
I know it,
I'll make sure you know.

You pinched me,
I know it,
And now my eyes glow.

You tripped me,
I know it,
And you'll take a blow.

I'm angry,
I'm mad,
I'm upset,
It's bad.

Anger hits,
Anger hurts,
Anger yells,
Anger blurts.

Don't let it take you,
Don't let it grow,
Don't let it hurt you,
Let anger go.

Frustration

I'm sitting in math,
It looks all squiggly.
I'm in my chair,
But I'm getting wiggly.

This is too hard,
This is just crazy,
Don't call me stupid!
Don't call me lazy!

I want to get it,
Really I do,
But it is so long,
Does it make sense to you?

I'm sitting in reading,
It looks all wrong,
I'm on the carpet,
But I can't sit long.

This is too hard,
This is just crazy,

Don't call me stupid!
Don't call me lazy!

I want to read,
Really I do,
But words look like noodles,
Does it make sense to you?

I guess I'm frustrated,
I don't understand,
Could you please help me?
Please take my hand.

Sadness

One day, she left,
My cat named Kitty.

She was so fluffy,
She was so pretty.

One day, she left,
And now I am here.

She was the best,
She always sat near.

One day, she left.
Now what to do?

She was my friend,
Played with me, too.

One day, she left,
Then came the tears.

She used to snuggle,

She stopped my fears.

Today, I sit,
All by myself.

I see her toy,
Up on the shelf.

Today, I cry,
Sit on the rug.

I see her bed,
Give it a hug.

Today, I hide,
It's nice and dark.

I see her window,
The scratches she'd mark.

Today, I'm sad,
No way around it.

For now, I am lost,
But I'll come out of it.

FEAR!

I was walking
Down hall
When I saw
Something crawl.

It was big,
It was hairy,
It was mean,
It was SCARY!

I ran screaming,
Yelled so much,
Tripped on stairs,
Fell a bunch.

I was shaking
In my shoes
When I saw
Something move.

It was huge,
It was sneaky,

It was red,

It was CREEPY!

I ran screaming,

Eyes so wide,

Tried to find,

A place to hide.

I was hiding

In my room

When I saw

Something zoom.

It was tall,

It was grimy,

It was blue,

It was SLIMY!

Sometimes we can get so scared

We don't look to see what's there.

Sometimes toys have scary faces

If they sit in the wrong places.

So take a look

And don't get scared.
No need to fear
There's nothing there.

Grumpy

I don't want to,
Don't ask me,
I don't want to,
Let me be.

I'm not mad,
I'm not sad,
I'm not bored,
I'm not glad.

I'm just grumpy,
Feelings all lumpy.

I don't like it,
Yes, it's true,
I don't like it,
I *used* to.

I'm not sleepy,
I'm not crazy,
I'm not goofy,
I'm not lazy.

I'm just grumpy,
Feelings all lumpy.

When you don't know what to feel,
And you just want to snap,
You don't want to smile,
You don't want to clap,

Know that it's okay,
We all get this way.

When you can't get all happy,
And you just want to frown,
You don't want to play,
You don't want to clown,

Know that it's okay,
We all get this way.
Sometimes we just get grumpy,
Riding feelings can get bumpy.

8 POEMS ABOUT SCHOOL

First Day

It's my first day,
My first day at school.

I check out my shoes,
Make sure they look cool.

It's my first day,
And I am so excited.

I peek into the room,
I smile, I can't hide it.

It's my first day,
And I go find my seat.

It is by my friend,
And I think that's neat.

It's my first day,
And it is all so new.

I look up at the teacher,
To see what we will do.

It's my first day,
New shirt, new shorts, new hair.
I feel like I look good,
Like a superhero would.

It's my first day,
I know that I'm so smart.

And on this first day,
I am ready to start.

Teacher

Look, it's the teacher!
They look so tall.

Look, it's the teacher!
And now I feel small.

Will they like me?
Are they kind?
I talk soft,
Will they mind?

Will they be good?
Are they fast?
I need help,
Will I last?

Look, it's the teacher!
They smile at me.

Look, it's the teacher!
And now I feel free.

I will talk soft,

They will be kind,

I will need help,

And they won't mind.

I will be fast,

They will be cool,

I can go slow,

Hey, I love school!

Look, it's a teacher!

A helper on the way.

Look, it's a teacher!

I know they'll save the day.

My Desk

I have a desk,
It's at the back.

The top is brown,
The legs are black.

It has a lid,
It just lays there.

It has a scratch,
But I don't care.

Inside is stuff,
And it's all mine.

It's all a mess,
But it is fine.

There is a book,
And then a pen.

A paper, too,

I look again.

I find some gum,
And then a stick.

There is a toy,
I hide it quick!

The lid is stuck,
The teacher looks.

I push the toy,
I grab my books.

I shut the lid,
I look up fast.

The teacher talks,
I made it past!
My desk is old,
It's kind of rusty.

But it holds lots,
My desk is trusty.

Carpet Time

We go to the carpet,
We sit in a square.

We go to the carpet,
Teacher's in a chair.

We go to the carpet,
It is time to read.

We go to the carpet,
Learn the things we need.

We go to the carpet,
Sit and try to see.

We go to the carpet,
Hope they call on me!

Carpet time is funny,
We get to make noise.

Carpet time is busy,

We can play with toys.

Carpet time is chatty,
We can talk sometimes.

Carpet time is sitting,
Learn to count the dimes.

Carpet time is happy,
We can sit by friends.

Carpet time is so cool,
Hope it never ends!

Class Time

I come in,
I sit down.
Read my book,
Then I frown.

What is next?
What to do.
I look up,
Find a clue!

First is math,
Next we leave,
Off to art
Or P.E.!

Then we read,
Take a break,
Pick our lunch,
What to take?

Read aloud
Is the best,

Science time,

Last a test!

Math class time

Is so cool.

We make shapes

And count, too.

Art is fun,

Learn to color.

P.E.'s neat,

Tag each other.

Books we read

Wait on shelves.

I see princes,

I see elves.

Teacher reads,

Reads some more,

It is super,

Not a bore.

Science time's

Kind of nuts!

Make a mess,

Poke at stuff.

What a day!

Lots to do!

Let's get started!

See what's new!

9 POEMS ABOUT FOOD

Salad

I look at my plate,
What is that I see?

Kind of looks like grass…
But that cannot be.

Then I see a red thing,
Round and slimy, too.

You say it's tomato,
But I just say, "Ew!"

There is a white river
Falling down the grass.

You tell me it's ranch,
But I think I'll pass.

Then I find an orange stick,
Sitting in the goo.

That is called a carrot?
And I eat that, too?

No, you must be crazy,
This is not for me.
I do not eat salads,
I'm a kid, you see?

You want me to try that?
Put it to my lips?

Open up and take it?
Can't I lick the tip?

Fine, I guess I'll just try,
See what it's about…

Hey, it's kind of tasty!
I'm glad that I found out!

Candy

It's sweet,
It's sticky,
It's great,
Never icky.

I eat it,
Every day,
Grab some more,
But you say,

"Not so much,
That's too many,
You can't eat
So much candy!"

But it's sweet,
But it's sticky,
But it's great,
Never icky.

I eat more,
I can't stop,

Grab some more,
Lick my chops.

"You must stop,
Yes, you should,
No more now,
It's not good!"

Still it's sweet,
Still it's sticky,
Still it's great,
Never icky.

I just eat,
Eat all day,
But then I
Want to play.

"Hey, what's wrong?
I can't do things,
I can't run,
And I can't sing!"

It was sweet,

It was sticky,
It was great,
But I feel icky.

I'm too big,
I'm not happy,
I can't move,
I get snappy.

Candy's good,
Something to eat,
But just some,
Make it a treat.

Fruit

What is this yellow thing?
It's all thin and long.

This is a banana!
Peel it, bite it, gone.

What is this orange ball?
It's all soft and round.

This is called an orange!
It is sweet, I found.

What is this shiny thing?
It's all hard and red.

This is called an apple!
It's juicy, I said.

What is this big green ball?
It's stripes are up and down.

This is watermelon!

It grows on the ground.

What is this spiky stuff?
It's got lots of pokes.

This is pineapple!
It's so good, no joke.

What are these tiny things?
Blue and round and small.

These are called blueberries!
You could eat them all.

Snacks

Snack attack!

Did you see?
There are chips
Staring at me.

Snack attack!

Did you know?
See cookies,
Have to go.

Snack attack!

Did you guess?
Sweets for me
Are the best.

Snack attack!

Did you buy?
Got it all,

I can't lie.

Snack attack!

Did you look?
Got some pop,
Didn't cook.

Snack attack!

Did you peek?
Ate some cake
Each day this week.

Snack attack!

Snacks got me!
I'm too full,
Can't you see?

I need a meal,
But I feel,
Full of snacks.
Can't go back.

Snacks are cool,
Snacks at school,
Snacks you smash,
But then you crash.

Pick a fruit,
Pick a veggie,
Grab a snack,
But not just any.

My Plate

It is time to eat,
Look down at my plate,
It is time to eat,
And I cannot wait.

It is time to eat,
I see lots to pick,
It is time to eat,
Better do it quick!

It is time to eat,
First my fruits and veggies,
It is time to eat,
I don't take too many.

It is time to eat,
Meat is what I see,
It is time to eat,
Just a bit for me.

It is time to eat,
Maybe I have bread,

It is time to eat,
Have to use my head.

It is time to eat,
Maybe I have sweets,
It is time to eat,
Those are special treats.

It is time to eat,
Look down at my plate.
It is time to eat,
And I cannot wait.

10 POEMS ABOUT SHARING AND CARING

Sharing

First it's you,
Then it's me,
That is sharing
How it should be.

First I hold,
Then you hold,
That is sharing,
So I'm told.

First you go,
Then I go,
That is sharing,
That I know.

First I cross,
Then you cross,
That is sharing,

Don't be a boss.

First you zoom,
Then I zoom,
That is sharing
In my room.

First I read,
Then you read,
That is sharing,
Just what we need.

First you ride,
Then a ride,
That is sharing,
That I've tried.

First I play,
Then you play,
That is sharing,
Do it all day.

First you swing,
Then I swing,

That is sharing,
The best thing.

Taking Turns

You go first,
You go last,
It's okay,
We'll have a blast.

We take turns,
Because it's fair
We must take turns,
It's everywhere.

We wait in line,
We raise our hand,
Taking turns,
It's what we planned.

You get to go,
No matter what,
So wait your turn,
Please don't say, "But!"

There is no "but."
We must take turns.

We all will go.
We all must learn.

And if your turn,
It never comes,
Just try again,
You will get some.

We all need turns,
It keeps things cool,
So wait your turn,
When you're at school.

And wait your turn,
Just wait awhile,
Just wait your turn,
With a big smile.

Giving

This is for you,
I hope it will do.

I wanted to make it,
I tried not to break it.

It is not much,
But I worked a bunch.

I want you to have it,
It's kind of a rabbit.

I used lots of sticks,
Ones that I picked.

There's glitter and glue,
It's red, yellow, blue.

I made it with pink,
Your favorite, I think.

I have worked so hard,

And here, I made a card.

I wrote that inside,
I wrote it, I tried.

Please hold out your hand,
And watch my gift land.

This is all for you,
I hope it will do.

I give and feel good,
I give just like I should.

Helping

Let me help you,
I am here,
Let me help you,
Have no fear.

Let me help you,
It's okay.
Let me help you,
Every day.

Let me help you,
Help is great.
Let me help you,
Not too late.

I don't need help,
I am smart.
I don't need help,
Don't you start.

I don't need help,
I can do it.

I don't need help,
I'll just do it.

I don't need help,
Help is bad,
I don't need help,
Makes me mad.

We all need help,
Even you,
We all need help,
Yes, we do.

I don't need help,
Help is lame!

But when you're stuck,
Who's to blame?

Find some help,
Please don't frown.
Help is there,
When you fall down.

Caring

I see my friends around me,
They all stop and smile,
And with my friends around me,
I can rest awhile.

My friends will now take care of me,
My friends are good and kind, you see.

When I need care,
My friends are there,
That makes me so happy.

I see a friend who needs me,
I stop and help them out,
And when that friend is better,
We go play about.

My friend is now able to rest,
Caring for friends is what is best.

When they need care,
Then I am there,

So put me to the test.

I see my friends around me,
They will be right here,
And we care for each other,

Final